151

Quick Ideas
for
Start-Up
Entrepreneurs

James L. Silvester

CAREER PRESS   The Career Press, Inc.
Franklin Lakes, NJ

Copyright © 2007 by James L. Silvester

151 QUICK IDEAS FOR START-UP ENTREPRENEURS
EDITED BY KATE HENCHES
TYPESET BY GINA TALUCCI
Cover design by Jeff Piasky
Printed in the U.S.A. by Book-mart Press

To order this title, please call toll-free 1-800-CAREER-1 (NJ and Canada: 201-848-0310) to order using VISA or MasterCard, or for further information on books from Career Press.

CAREER
PRESS

The Career Press, Inc., 3 Tice Road, PO Box 687,
Franklin Lakes, NJ 07417
www.careerpress.com

Library of Congress Cataloging-in-Publication Data
Silvester, James L.
  151 quick ideas for start-up entrepreneurs / by James L. Silvester
    p. cm.
  Includes index.
  ISBN-13: 978-1-56414-957-2
  ISBN-10: 1-56414-957-9
  1. New business enterprises. 2. Small business—Management.
  I. Title. II. Title: One hundred fifty one quick ideas for start-up entrepreneurs.

HD62.5S5559 2007
658.1'1--dc22

2007041033

Contents

How to Use This Book   **9**
Introduction   **11**
1. Breathing Space Is Necessary   13
2. Never Enough Outlets   13
3. The Right Executive Chair   14
4. Prioritize Equipment Usage   15
5. Keep Those Files Close   16
6. Tax Deductions   16
7. Home Deductions   17
8. Improving Human Relations
   Within the Entrepreneurial Firm   18
9. Learn to Listen   20
10. Employees Are Assets   21
11. Set the Bar   22
12. Control Your Inventory and Thrive   23
13. Get a Handle on Your Numbers   24
14. Don't Hire Uncle Fred   25
15. Being Your Own Boss, and Someone Else's   26
16. No White Lies   27
17. Wireless Is Priceless   28
18. Don't Be a Chump   29
19. E-mail You Way to Success   30

20.	The "New" Cash Register	31
21.	Does Not Compute	32
22.	Organize Your Data	33
23.	Inventory Management the Easy Way	34
24.	Always Monitor	35
25.	Don't Risk the Family Farm	37
26.	Protect Thyself With a Business Condom	38
27.	Build That Insurance Program Now	39
28.	Business Interruption Insurance	40
29.	Key Person Insurance	41
30.	Criminal Insurance	42
31.	The Four Basics of Insurance	42
32.	General Liability	43
33.	Product/Service Liability	44
34.	Home-Based Business Insurance	45
35.	Internet Business Insurance	45
36.	Malpractice Insurance	46
37.	Workers' Compensation	47
38.	Using Insurance for Funding	48
39.	Borrow Wisely	49
40.	Equity Financing	50
41.	Uncle Fred Can Be a Pain	51
42.	Suppliers Can Be Lenders	52
43.	Lenders Are Really Snake Oil Vendors	53
44.	Not All Money Is the Same	54
45.	Marketing or Bust	55
46.	Expand Upon Your Base	56
47.	Judging the Markets	57
48.	Give Them What They Want	58
49.	Market Consideration	59

50. Competitive Consideration — 60
51. Managing the Market Mix — 61
52. Don't Forget Customer Needs — 63
53. Market Testing or Die — 63
54. Marketing Data on the Cheap — 65
55. Opportunities Galore — 66
56. Steps in the Marketing Research Process — 67
57. A Customer Relations Policy Is Money
in the Bank — 70
58. The Customer Is King — 71
59. Trial and Error — 72
60. Market Promotion and Strategy — 73
61. Controlling for Profits — 74
62. Income Tax Is a Fact of Life — 75
63. Estimated Tax — 76
64. Employment Taxes — 77
65. Excise Tax — 78
66. Controlled Impulsing — 79
67. The Cash Flow Blues — 80
68. Fall in Love With the Wastebasket — 81
69. High Pay-Off Actions — 82
70. Important Versus Urgent — 83
71. Interruptions Galore — 84
72. Results Versus Tasks — 85
73. Technology Time Management — 86
74. Putting Your Finger on Time-Wasters — 87
75. Time-Wasters — 88
76. Prioritizing Time to Get Things Done — 89
77. Desire to Win — 90
78. Letting It Rip — 92

79.	Motivate Yourself to Success	93
80.	Taking the Bull by the Horns	94
81.	Capital	95
82.	Channels of Distribution Are Key	95
83.	Beware of Global Warming	97
84.	Competitors Are Really Sharks	99
85.	Credit Policies Are a Must	100
86.	Delivery as a Business Process	100
87.	Economic Climate, Not the Weather	101
88.	Financial Control or Die	103
89.	Government Regulation Is Costly	103
90.	Industry Trends Are Important	104
91.	Inflation Risks Are Real	105
92.	International Events Cannot Be Avoided	106
93.	Labor Is Expensive	108
94.	Licensing Is Necessary	109
95.	Market Research Must Be Done	110
96.	Operations Policy Helps Manage	111
97.	Pricing for Success	112
98.	Product/Service Will Dictate Success	113
99.	Raw Materials Are Important for Some	114
100.	Research and Development Is an Investment	115
101.	State of Technology and Your Business	116
102.	Storage Is Important	117
103.	TopographyMay Limit Your Options	118
104.	Trade Credit as a Managing Tool	119
105.	Vendors Are Not Your Friends	120
106.	Vendors May Squeal	121
107.	War on Margins	122
108.	Warranties Are Real Promises	124

109.	Road Map to Success	125
110.	Are You a Good Decision-Maker	126
111.	Common Decision-Making Mistakes	128
112.	Excellence Pays Dividends	129
113.	We Be Metric	131
114.	Managing Cash and Credit	133
115.	Managing Growth the Right Way	136
116.	Never Say Never	137
117.	Organize Yourself	139
118.	Set Your Goals Now	140
119.	Short-Term Suicide	141
120.	Sweat Buys Equity	142
121.	10 Steps to Wise Decision-Making	144
122.	Truth or Consequences	145
123.	Technology Assessment Planning	147
124.	Technology Is a Must	148
125.	Websites Are a Must Nowadays	150
126.	Always Compare	151
127.	Tweak It to Death	152
128.	Update Your Plan	152
129.	Cheerleaders Wanted	153
130.	Play the Game	154
131.	A Thank You Goes a Long Way	155
132.	Bragging Rights	156
133.	Make That Call	156
134.	It's Nice to Have Friends	157
135.	Kiss the Booty	158
136.	Become an Idea Generator in Three Easy Steps	159
137.	Creative Thinking Techniques	160

138.	Calculating the Risk Factor	161
139.	Go for It	162
140.	New Ideas Are Money in the Bank	163
141.	Never Say You're Sorry	165
142.	Developing Ideas	166
143.	No Profits Without Risk	168
144.	Protecting Your Flanks	169
145.	Setting up the Innovative and Creative Environment	170
146.	The Secrets	171
147.	Ushering in the New Era	172
148.	War on Markets	174
149.	U.S. Small Business Administration	175
150.	University Business Development Centers	176
151.	SCORE and ACE	177
Index		**179**
About the Author		**187**

How to Use This Book

Every quick idea in this book has been selected to directly or indirectly help you gain and retain customers, create relationships, and build a successful business.

Don't try to implement all 151 ideas at once, because some won't be a good fit right now. Read through all 151 quick ideas and select only those that can really make a difference.

Label your ideas:

* Implement now.

* Review again in 30 days.

* Pass the idea along to _____.

Involve your staff in selecting and implementing these ideas, and don't forget to give credit for their successes! Invest in additional copies of this book and distribute them to your staff. Get everyone involved in selecting and recommending various quick ideas.

Revisit this book every 90 days. As your business changes, you will find new quick ideas that might suit you better now that competition is heating up.

Remember: All the ideas in this book have been proven in businesses across the United States and around the world. They have worked for others and will work for you!

Introduction

If you have ever thought about starting your own business, you've got lots of company and *151 Quick Ideas for Start-Up Entrepreneurs* is perfect for you.

The United States Department of Labor states that by the year 2010 there will be more self-employed people than those that hold traditional "wage-slave" jobs.

A recent poll suggests that 90 percent of those between the ages of 25 and 44 want to own a small business. A recent government study shows that the largest demographic group starting small businesses is the Baby Boomers. Seventeen percent of Boomers are starting businesses and they represent a massive block of people.

There are many reasons for this entrepreneurial surge. Some do it to supplement their existing income; some do it because they don't have enough retirement income to sustain them. Some have lost their jobs and do it out of economic necessity, others because they want to break the chains of wage-slavery, and still others because there is no more security left in Corporate America.

Every quick idea in this book has been selected to directly or indirectly help you gain and retain customers, create relationships, and build a successful business. All the ideas in this book have been proven in businesses across the United States and around the world. They have worked for others and will work for you!

Just remember: a resource is only as good as your willingness to use it. In today's complex, competitive, and ever-changing business environment, education and information resources are very important. In fact, education is a lifelong endeavor. Make it an adventure and make some money at the same time.

1

Breathing Space Is Necessary

The space you choose for your home office should be illuminated and properly ventilated, with enough room for furniture, supplies, storage compartments, and other items you use on a regular basis. Windows are great for natural light and that all-important "inspiration," but they can just as easily be a persistent distraction. It may be best to configure your work area so that the windows are behind you or to the side.

Assignment
Make it a comfortable place to which you want to go to when you wake up in the morning.

Epilogue
Constantly evaluate the space to ensure it meets your needs.

2

Never Enough Outlets

Your home office should also be equipped with sufficient electrical outlets to safely support your office equipment and appliances, as well as connections for your telephone, fax and internet access. Any costs incurred to add outlets and any other utilities to your office (for example, heating and air-conditioning ducts) are tax deductible.

Assignment

Local code may demand an upgrade for a home office. Check with your local zoning and planning. Don't use extension cords. You are inviting a fire.

Epilogue

Keep an eye on your power needs and adjust appropriately.

3

The Right Executive Chair

Consider what kind of furniture you'll need for your business, including file cabinets, printer stands, and any other items needed to organize records, tools, and supplies. Browse catalogs or measure furniture you already have and compare those dimensions with the available space in your office. This will make it easier to find an ideal layout without the risk of discovering, too late, that your new desk doesn't fit.

Assignment

Plan ahead and buy wisely. Many office furniture outlets, including the discount catalog companies, have home-office planning aids. Use them to avoid costly mistakes.

Epilogue

Leave some space in the budget to update and add furnishings as needed.

4

Prioritize Equipment Usage

Follow the same process described in Idea 3 with the equipment you will use, whether it's a computer and a fax or machining equipment. You will almost certainly use some things less frequently than others, so consider ways to place these items so that they're convenient, yet out of the way.

Assignment

Prioritize equipment use to better serve your business needs and maximize space.

Epilogue

Keep the frequently used equipment close and the not so frequently used equipment somewhat close but not in the way.

15

5

Keep Those Files Close

Avoid moving any business equipment or files out of your home office. You cannot afford to waste time tracking down misplaced tools or research information, especially when a deadline is near. And if customers visit your home office, an organized work environment will say a lot about you and the quality of your services. Even if you never have visitors, taking a few moments to straighten up at the end of the day gives you a head start on tomorrow's tasks.

Assignment

Avoid irritations by having your files close when needed and your work environment clean and organized.

Epilogue

There is nothing more annoying than trying to find a "rogue" file when needed or digging through a pile of papers on a messy desk searching for a document.

6

Tax Deductions

The Internal Revenue Service will let you deduct expenses related only to that part of your home that you use *exclusively and regularly* for business. This includes the mortgage/rent cost of floor space, utilities, and furnishings for areas where you actually perform your business and customer reception or meeting areas. You may also deduct expenses for parts of your home used as a daycare facility, or to store inventory you sell in your business—even if

> ### Assignment
>
> Although discussed more in detail later in this book, even a micro-business operating out of a home basement needs to be sensitive to the taxman.

you sometimes use those areas for personal purposes as well. Consult the IRS Website at *www.IRS.gov*.

> ### Epilogue
>
> *Be able to justify every deduction.*

7

Home Deductions

In the past, it was true that taking a home-office deduction on your income taxes was a red flag to the Internal Revenue Service. No more. The growing bulge of home-based small enterprises is a fact of life. The government is now actively promoting home-based entrepreneurial businesses as an economic policy. So, don't be afraid to take that home-office deduction. But be diligent and fair to Uncle Sam.

For example, if you live in a 2,000-square-foot house and you use your family room in the basement as a home office, and it is

<table>
<tr><td>

Assignment

Take stock of your physical living layout in your home and pick a couple of places where you could locate your office. Evaluate the pros and cons of each. Pick the best alternative.

</td></tr>
</table>

400 square feet, you are in essence using 20 percent of your home living area as business-generating floor space. So if your total housing costs including your mortgage, utilities, insurance, taxes, and so on, is $20,000 per year, your gross deduction would be $4,000 and reported on Schedule C of your tax return. However, to play it safe, it would be wise to determine how many hours a day you actually generate income in that home office space. Let's say it's 8 hours per day and the additional 16 hours is used for personal use. That would reduce your deduction to $1,333, and would be better able to survive IRS scrutiny should they decide to take a look. But if the space is used "exclusively" to generate your income and not used for personal purpose, the $4,000 would be justified and would survive an audit.

Epilogue

Keep your office contained to that room to prevent losing files in other parts of the house.

8

Improving Human Relations Within the Entreprenurial Firm

Tips:

1. Improve your own general understanding of human behavior.

18

2. Accept the fact that others do not always see things as you do.

3. In any differences of opinion, consider the possibility that you may not have the right answer.

4. Show your employees that you are interested in them and that you want their ideas on how conditions can be improved.

5. Treat your employees as individuals; never deal with them impersonally.

6. Respect difference of opinion.

7. Provide information and guidance on matters affecting employees' security.

8. Express appreciation publicly for jobs well done.

9. Offer criticism privately, in the form of constructive suggestions for improvement.

> **Assignment**
> Employees are your most valuable assets. Treat them accordingly.

10. Train supervisors to be concerned about the people they supervise, the same as they would be about merchandise or materials or equipment.

11. Keep your staff up-to-date on matters that affect them.

12. Quell false rumors, and provide correct information.

13. Be fair!

Epilogue

Create a comfortable and respectable workplace. This is called "Organizational Hygiene."

9

Learn to Listen

Do you know that most divorces occur because of the lack of communication between spouses? Likewise, many employer/employee partings are due to communication voids within organizations. You must give your employees the opportunity to express their feelings, ideas, and viewpoints. This must be done in an environment absent of fear and retaliation. But this is a two-lane highway. Not only must you develop a work environment that allows freedom of expression, you must not be fearful of what your employees have to say. Employees are generally a valuable source of information. For reasons that cannot be easily explained, you will find that your employees will see things that you do not. Opportunities and cost-saving methods are, at times, very apparent to employees, but not to the entrepreneur.

Assignment

Listen, listen, and listen more. Employees want to be heard and taken seriously. Give them your time and patience, even if they complain about small issues.

Epilogue

Listen to your employees and treat them well.

10

Employees Are Assets

Employees are your most important resource. As an entrepreneur you will soon realize that salary and wages will be your single largest expense factor. The way in which you manage your human resources will determine the degree to which you are successful as an entrepreneur. In other words, human productivity will make or break you. It's not an easy resource to manage. Research has shown that about 75 percent of all workers are unhappy with their jobs. In addition, entrepreneurial firms have fewer resources per employee than do larger companies. Consequently, this complicates the employee morale problems for small enterprises.

Once you realize that employees are income generators after reaching a certain level of output, you will note that it is impossible to survive without them. Another factor you must consider is the growing employee shortages that are starting to appear throughout the country in all occupational classifications. This is due to the stable economy. Enhanced employment-related competition among all employers will make it difficult and costly to keep good employees. That doesn't make life simpler for the new or existing entrepreneur.

Assignment

Write down your description of a good employee and how those characteristics can benefit both your business and the employee.

21

> **Epilogue**
> *Create a job description and job expectations for each employee, and reevaluate them every 180 days.*

11

Set the Bar

Incentives are the foundation of America's economic system and standard of living. The tax incentives provided in 2003 are largely responsible for our current state of prosperity. They fostered a powerful drive to succeed and to profit.

This brings to mind a consulting project in which I participated as consultant-in-charge. The project was classified as a "turnaround" due to the nature of the difficulties that we faced. What really surprised me was that this enterprise was managed by a very intelligent entrepreneur who never gave thought to the notion of employee incentives. When I mentioned the possibility of implanting incentive systems, the idea was initially dismissed as "too expensive."

The entrepreneur and I had a meeting with the employees. They were informed of the need to work harder. For their cooperation and enhanced productivity, we promised that they would share in cost savings and

> ### Assignment
>
> Query your employees and accountant for their input about an incentive program. Experiment with different systems and pick the one that suits the best interests of your business and employees.

profits. An incentive bonus system was established, and the rest is history. Productivity and earning soared. The company began to generate $10,000 to $20,000 a month in profits. Some of the employees earned an amount equal to 25 percent of their annual salaries in the form of performance bonuses.

Epilogue

Make sure you stick with the plan you create and review it annually for needed modifications.

12

Control Your Inventory and Thrive

Assignment

Create a manageable and effective inventory-control system that works for your particular firm. There are many inexpensive software programs available at places such as Office Max to accomplish this task.

Proper inventory management can mean the difference between profit or loss, and, in some cases, survival. Excessive inventories will lock up needed cash that would otherwise be used to generate sales and profits.

Whatever inventory procedure is implemented, the cost of the endeavor must be less than its potential savings. Excessive inventory control can inflict the same harm as too little. A balance must be struck. The optimum solution is hard to find, but it is imperative if the business is to manage resources correctly.

There are complex statistical methods used to determine optimum inventory levels. Discussion of these are beyond the scope of this book. Therefore, seek out a competent business consultant when faced with inventory problems. Talking with other business owners who have faced similar difficulties may provide a wealth of helpful information. Also, seeking out college professors with specialties in the field of information sciences may prove to be useful in solving problems related to inventory control.

Epilogue

Take a physical inventory at specific intervals to keep your inventory under control.

13

Get a Handle on Your Numbers

Existing and prospective small business owners should attempt to understand the financial complexities involved in business operations. A thorough understanding of financial statements (balance sheet, profit and loss statement, and cash flow statement) will provide a solid foundation for making good business decisions. These statements, showing all revenue, expense, asset, and liability accounts, should be prepared and examined once a month by a competent accountant and reviewed by the firm's owner(s). Each account within the statements should be shown for the current period and the same period for last year. In addition, current year-to-date totals can be given for financial control purposes.

Good financial statements will also serve to contain costs. Studying past and present information concerning cost accounts may provide valuable insight into the conditions affecting expense figures. Also, an examination of revenue accounts may indicate the degree of product/service mark-up or mark-down required to maintain adequate levels of sales and

Assignment

You will be surprised how little it costs for an accounting service to do monthly financial statements: It is approximately $100 per month for most small firms.

profits. It may show a need to alter existing lines through modification, new introductions, and/or phase-out.

Epilogue

Strive to produce monthly financial statements, even if you have someone else do them.

14

Don't Hire Uncle Fred

Nepotism is as old as work itself. And it will continue as long as the "good ole boy" network remains intact. Now, there are some firms that have tried to deal with nepotism through various screening processes and have met with success. However, the vast majority of companies are still plagued with it. Smaller firms seem more inclined to tolerate nepotism for obvious reasons. Many are family operated enterprises anyway. It is called the "Blood Is Thicker Than Water" syndrome. Even though you may be appalled by such activity, upon becoming an entrepreneur, you too may be lured or forced to accommodate nepotism as a way of life.

Assignment

If you can't avoid mixing family with business, create and explain rules on how the family relationships will work within the business and make no exceptions to the rules.

Epilogue

The non-family employees will be watching, so be fair to everyone.

15

Being Your Own Boss, and Someone Else's

If you are very successful at your home-based enterprise, you may find the need to hire additional help to facilitate the growth of the business. You then face the choice of paying people as "independent contractors" or as "employees." The differences can be very large and pose a few financial risks.

Your instinctive reaction is going to be to pay people as independent contractors and report their earnings on IRS Form 1099. You might be saving some dollars because you don't have to pay their social security taxes, workers compensation insurance premiums, unemployment insurance, and the expense of collecting, forwarding, and accounting for federal and state tax withholding.

It's always safe to pay people as employees, and the expenses are all deductible just like independent contractor expenses. You will have to pay 50 percent of their social security taxes, pay workers' compensation insurance, and pay unemployment insurance premiums. All in all, it will add a 15- to 20-percent cost burden over paying these people as independent contractors.

Assignment

Check the IRS Website at *www.Irs.Gov/Businesses/Index.Html*. They have criteria concerning declaring whether a person is an "employee" or "independent contractor."

Epilogue
Check with your CPA or tax attorney to play it safe.

16

No White Lies

Never (and I emphasize *never*) lie to your employees. It's like lying to the media—they never forget. Some managers feel that there are economic benefits to be gained from not telling the truth to their employees. Some justify their actions by rationalizing that, if lying is for the good of the system or organization, it is okay to do. This process can become contagious, and, if you consistently utilize this tactic, it will come home to haunt you. Employee loyalty and morale will be affected in a negative way. Lying will cost you more

27

in terms of lost productivity and employee turnover than any gains that could ever be realized. And—you never know—it could even attract media attention!

Assignment

Foster an atmosphere of honesty between yourself and your employees, and let them know you're sticking to it.

Epilogue

Never lie to your employees.

17

Wireless Is Priceless

Are you tripping over cords all over your office? Are your peripheral cords so tangled there is no hope of separating them? If you answered yes to either of these questions, it may be time to go wireless.

One wireless gateway or router can support up to 25 computers. This should be more than enough for a small

Assignment

It's still possible to trip over a cord and break your neck, and we all know that hurts. Break the wire habit. Once you go wireless, you will never go back.

business office. If you plan on adding more computers to your office, you can simply add on in the future or purchase an extra gateway in advance.

Once you have purchased your gateway, place it in a central location in your office. The normal range for a gateway in an office environment is 75 to 100 feet. The further your computer is from the gateway, the more you'll notice something called "gradual degradation." This means that the speed of your network will not be as fast in computers located furthest from the gateway.

After setting up, your new wireless network will be ready to use. If you want to add a printer to your network, you can either purchase a network-enabled printer that connects by Ethernet cable, or a Wi-Fi–capable printer. Once they're on your network, all your computers will be able to share a single printer.

Epilogue
The convenience, portability, and reduced expense of going wireless maks it well worth it.

18

Don't Be a Chump

Other important aspects of business expense are who the money is getting paid to, how you are getting the money to them, for what purpose, and how often. Overpayment is a plight in many businesses because of poor and outdated bookkeeping practices. A program such as Quicken or

Assignment

Have a fool-proof way to keep track of your expenses and enter everything as quickly as possible into your accounting system.

QuickBooks can handle your company's check writing, payroll calculation, and payment, and maintain all your vendor and supplier payments. It also gives you the ability to print out your own invoices as any professional business should. Most accounting programs also come with tax calculation capability so you'll know to how much of your hard earned money Uncle Sam and your state are entitled.

Epilogue

Keep track of everything. You never know when you might need that receipt. It could be six months from now, or even six years from now.

19

E-mail Your Way to Success

E-mail marketing is one of the most effective ways to keep in touch with customers. It is generally cost-effective, and, if done properly, can help build brand awareness and loyalty. At a typical cost of only a few cents per message, it's a bargain compared to traditional direct mail at $1 or more per piece. In addition, response rates on e-mail marketing are strong, ranging from 0.5 percent to 3 percent depending on the industry and format. Response

Assignment

E-mailing to a "targeted list" or a "captive list," such as your existing customers, can produce great results. In addition to pure marketing, try a monthly "newsletter" directed to your customers, vendors, and others who may have an interest in your business. Only good will come out of those efforts.

rates for traditional mail averages in the 1 to 3 percent range. One of the benefits of e-mail marketing is the demographic information that customers provide when communicating with you. Discovering who your customers really are—their ages, gender, incomes, and special interests—can help you target your products and services to their needs.

Epilogue

Watch out for "spam." Don't send unsolicited e-mails. Some states will throw you in jail for sending junk e-mails.

20

The "New" Cash Register

If you are a retail business owner, then a computerized cash register is a must, but your register doesn't have to be a computer. Let me explain this. You could get a register that is, in and of itself, a computer that keeps track of all related files for you, and this is the route you would want to take if you have more than one register operating at one time. However, you could also go with an inexpensive register, such as a Sharp, that allows you to hook into a computer and pull the records out of its memory. This will make logging your daily numbers into that spreadsheet (that you should be

Assignment

In a non-retail setting you still need technology for tracking sales. Even wholesalers have "cash registers," generally configured differently than retail operations.

31

keeping) even easier and more reliable as it's not going to depend on the human element entering them (and maybe missing a decimal point). Either of these solutions will allow you to keep an up-to-the minute grasp on your sales, on what merchandise is moving, and on tracking the time of your sales so you know when you are the busiest and during what times there are lulls.

Epilogue

Join the 21st century.

21

Does Not Compute

In today's business world, any serious attempt at a successful venture needs to include computerization or you may as well just keep the doors closed. Technology advances to make life easier and to get simple tasks done faster and make more complex situations easier to manage. Without spreadsheets to see where your finances are, databases to keep track of inventory, and a computerized register that can show you sales

Assignment

Start small with a computer system and let it grow with your business adding hardware and software as needed.

at the push of a button, you may as well go back to the dark ages of a 20-pound ledger and an inkwell to run your business. Remember, though, that technology is only as good as its uses and its users, so judge according to your needs and your capabilities as to what technology you bring in to your enterprise.

The best computer setup in the world does nothing for your business if you can't get it to do what you want, and it's not worth the price if you only need it for a few small functions. However, as with anything else you will decide on during your initial setup phase and later restructuring, leave room for upgrading your technology. Technology is probably the one area in your business plan on which you don't need to focus too far down the road. As technology advances and prices drop, it's almost always better to invest in new tech toys than to keep the old ones running.

Epilogue
Nowadays with prices very low, your investment will be returned quickly.

22

Organize Your Data

There are few things more frightening in the world than having a sit-down with an IRS agent when your records are incomplete, or—even worse—incorrect. As a business owner, you need to know where you capital is going, how much your business is earning, how much you're paying employees, vendors, and for municipal fees such as water and power. Of course you'll need to pay taxes on just about everything you do, so you need to have a way to put it all together. This sounds like a lot of different tasks to accomplish, and may require several programs, but for a small business these tasks can be performed quite easily with a bare bones PC setup, an office suite program, and an accounting application.

Because of the inexpensive prepackaged software available nowadays, it is simple to design a spreadsheet or database format using fixed columns and mathematical formulas. Once that is done, all you have to do is type the numbers in to calculate anything from daily to yearly results of your business. What once required new ledgers and logbooks and took untold hours compiling to truly get a grasp on your business standing, now can be compiled, recorded, and stored on a CD-ROM and able to be cross-referenced in no time flat. Want to know your

> ## Assignment
>
> A computer is only as good as a monkey behind the tube. Automate your office as much as you can, but know how to handle things manually as well, as a backup plan.

sales total on July 12th of last year? Just fire up that computer and take a look. Most new computer systems come with prepackaged Microsoft Excel, the granddaddy of all spreadsheet programs.

> ### Epilogue
> *As your technical experience matures, your need for manual control will lessen.*

23

Inventory Management the Easy Way

What good is a warehouse if you don't know what's in it or where a particular item is? With a good database and proper

Assignment

Put your toe in the water and start exploring some inventory control programs. They are not expensive and are available at such store as OfficeMax and Staples.

consistent usage of it, this knowledge won't be a problem for you. Technology, like a portable barcode reader linked to the master inventory database, can let you know what's come in, what's going out, what needs to be reordered, and what's not selling. If you're dealing with time-sensitive goods, you can keep on top of the dates you need to know. A computerized cash register can keep track of every barcode scanned through it to give you an accurate and reliable sales tracking system if you're in a retail business. Instead of having to log every delivery manually, and keeping those records stored in a box taking up space, wouldn't it be easier and better to just scan a barcode and use that time and space in a more profitable manner?

Epilogue

Look for "Retail Suite." It's a great little package for small retailers.

24

Always Monitor

Whether your business is in retail sales or not, whether you even handle money or merchandise in your business, you need to keep track of everything that goes on there. From cameras on the sales floor or in the warehouse, to those hanging over your employees' desks, you need to make sure that your time and money is not wasted. Your business depends on the people you have working for you who do their jobs during the time they are there, and those who sit around playing solitaire when they should be working. These individuals can cause huge financial losses, as not keeping an eye on your sales floor can also hurt. When goods find themselves walking out the door if no one's watching.

> ### Assignment
>
> Always monitor your business. There are inexpensive systems, both camera and computer, available to help you watch your operation.

Relax; you don't need to have your eyes glued to a little monitor watching over everything all the time. With a few cameras and a hard drive recorder you can check in whenever you want. If you set up your security with Web cams, you don't even have to be there to know what's happening back at work. If your business involves people using computers with Internet access, a monitoring program can keep them on task, and out of the chat rooms.

Epilogue
Remember, employee dishonesty costs the average small business 12 percent of its gross sales.

25

Don't Risk the Family Farm

Understanding risk is an important aspect of running any business. Some experts contend that an adequate insurance program, designed to reduce risk, is just as vital to the success of a firm as are other business functions. Without question, assets left unprotected could compromise the future existence of the business if loss occurred. Therefore, a sound risk reduction plan should be implemented and carefully managed to ensure economic viability in the event of loss due to unanticipated events.

Some insurance companies sell consolidated policies incorporating all coverage into one central agreement. In addition, many professional and trade associations have insurance products at discount group rates. For example, the National Small Business Association (located at 1604 K. Street, NW, Washington, DC 20006) provides some attractive insurance programs at reasonable prices.

Assignment

Always evaluate the firm's risk exposure on a timely and regular basis for purposes of upgrading or downgrading.

Epilogue

Periodic evaluation will ensure adequate coverage at reasonable cost, and, in some cases, the phasing-out of protection that has become unnecessary.

26

Protect Thyself With a Business Condom

Buying business insurance is among the best ways to prepare for the unexpected. Without proper "protection," misfortunes such as the death of a partner or key employee, embezzlement, a lawsuit, or a natural disaster could spell the end of a thriving operation.

Ranging from indispensable workers' compensation insurance to the relatively obscure executive kidnapping coverage, insurance is available for nearly any business risk.

Assignment

Take a look at your business and do a "risk analysis" to determine internal and external threats to your firm and insure accordingly.

Epilogue

Considering the multitude of available options, business owners must carefully weigh whether the cost of certain premiums will justify the coverage for a given risk.

27

Building That Insurance Program Now

Some recommendations:

* State the objective of the insurance plan.
* Try to deal with only one agent, if possible. Dealing with several may create confusion and disinformation.
* Assign responsibility for the program to one individual.
* Prevent or minimize losses through safety procedures and inspection procedures.
* State the potential for loss candidly. Failure to acquire needed coverage because of disinformation can be a threat to the viability of the firm.

> ### *Assignment*
>
> Structure an insurance program. A formalized plan outlining all aspects of the insurance program should be set forth for management purposes. Use these recommendations as your guide.

* No matter how small the chance for loss, all risks should be covered. Avoid underestimation of asset value to save money. If loss does occur, the firm may not recover its investment.
* Periodically, evaluate the insurance program to determine the need for modification. Some risk programs

have built-in automatic cost-of-living increases to protect against loss caused by increasing asset value due to inflation. All assets should be appraised occasionally to determine insurance requirements.

Epilogue

Always maintain adequate records concerning the risk reduction program. This information may be helpful later, when attempting to change or modify coverage.

28

Business Interruption Insurance

Assignment

You may be surprised to know that this happens often, in particular with changing and increasingly unpredictable weather patterns. Flooding, fire, and tornados are big issues. Evaluate your business according to its geographic area and locality, and insure yourself accordingly.

Some businesses may wish to acquire insurance that covers losses during natural disasters, fires, and other catastrophes that may cause the operation to shut down for a significant amount of time.

Epilogue

This insurance is not costly and will generally add about 15 percent to the overall cost to your policy. It's worth it.

29

Key Person Insurance

In addition to a business continuation plan that outlines how the company will maintain operations if a key person dies, falls ill, or leaves, some companies may wish to buy key-person insurance. This type of coverage is usually life insurance that names the corporation as a beneficiary if an essential person dies or is disabled.

Assignment

You want to be prepared and protect your loved ones and business partners should you become ill and/or die.

Epilogue

This insurance will provide the necessary funds to guarantee business continuity.

41

30

Criminal Insurance

No matter how tight security is in your workplace, theft and malicious damage are always possibilities. While the dangers associated with hacking, vandalism, and general theft are obvious, employee embezzlement is more common than most business owners think. Criminal insurance and employee bonds can provide protection against losses in most criminal areas.

Assignment

Some studies indicate that employee dishonesty costs businesses upwards of 12 percent of gross sales. Be diligent in screening your potential employees before hiring.

Epilogue

Require bonding when cash and other financial assets are handled by employees.

31

The Four Basics of Insurance

Four kinds of insurance are essential:

1. Fire insurance
2. Liability insurance

42

3.   Automobile insurance
4.   Workers' compensation insurance

In some areas, and in some kinds of businesses, criminal insurance, which is discussed in Idea 30, is also essential.

Assignment

Ask yourself the question: Am I certain that all the four points recited in Idea 31 have been given full consideration in my insurance program?

Epilogue

Constantly reevaluate your insurance needs.

32

General Liability

Many business owners buy general liability or umbrella liability insurance to cover legal hassles due to claims of negligence. These help protect against payments as the result of bodily injury or property damage, medical expenses, the cost of defending lawsuits, and settlement bonds or judgments required during an appeal procedure.

Assignment

This is the most basic of all insurance coverage. It is an absolute must-have for all small businesses. It provides only basic coverage, but it's a start to understanding and building a more comprehensive insurance program. I recommend, at least, the basics.

> **Epilogue**
> Many states and localities require this insurance for a business license.

33

Product/Service Liability

> **Assignment**
>
> This is a big "sue-happy" area. Everybody is claiming that products/services are harming their personal well-being. From the tobacco to the sunscreen industry, it's a hotbed of suit activity. Evaluate and see if it's right for you.

Companies that manufacture, wholesale, distribute, and retail a product may be liable for its safety. In addition, every service rendered may be capable of personal injury or property damage. Businesses are considered liable for negligence, breach of an express or implied warranty, defective products, and defective warnings or instructions.

> **Epilogue**
> Evaluate your product/service mix to determine the potential for suits and protect yourself accordingly.

34

Home-Based Business Insurance

Contrary to popular belief, homeowners' insurance policies do not generally cover home-based business losses. Commonly needed insurance areas for home-based businesses include business property, professional liability, personal and advertising injury, loss of business data, crime and theft, and disability.

Assignment

Yes, even if you operate out of your home, you need business insurance. Don't assume that your homeowners will cover a business risk. Some will and some won't. A few will insure partial business activities.

Epilogue

Don't assume anything, check with your insurance agent.

35

Internet Business Insurance

Web-based businesses may wish to look into specialized insurance that covers liability for damage done by hackers and viruses.

In addition, e-insurance often covers specialized online activities, including lawsuits resulting from meta tag abuse, banner advertising, or electronic copyright infringement.

Assignment

Technology can make a strange bedfellow. You need to protect yourself from the vulnerabilities created by the use of electronic commerce, which is becoming a growing national problem.

Epilogue

From information theft to a hacker crashing your Wesite and disrupting your business, you must be protected.

36

Malpractice Insurance

Assignment

As a member of the professional classes of our society, you must protect yourself from unwarranted lawsuits, and even those suits that may have merit, against you.

Some licensed professionals need protection against payments as the result of bodily injury or property damage, medical expenses, the cost of defending lawsuits, investigations and settlements, and bonds or judgments required during an appeal procedure.

> **Epilogue**
>
> *Love it or leave it, we live in a "sue-happy" society.*

37

Workers' Compensation

Required in almost every state, workers' compensation insurance pays for employees' medical expenses and missed wages if injured while working. The amount of insurance employers must carry, rate of payment, and what types of employees must be carried varies depending on the state. In most cases, business owners, independent contractors, domestic employees in private homes, farm workers, and unpaid volunteers are exempt.

Assignment

Workers' Compensation is the law in almost all states. The state does protect you if one of your employees gets injured on the job. Also, many independent contractors will attempt to collect on "workers' comp" if they are injured while working under contract for you. So, be sure you have those contractors actually qualify as contractors under IRS rules, and, once that is determined, make them sign waivers of insurance.

Epilogue

In absence of this, insure contractors and employees through another liability insurance policy.

38

Using Insurance for Funding

A standard feature of most life-insurance policies (except term insurance) is the owner's ability to borrow against the cash value of the policy. The money can be used for any business or personal need. It normally takes two years for a policy to accumulate sufficient cash value. You may borrow up to 95 percent of the cash value of the policy for an indefinite period of time. As long as you continue to pay the insurance premiums, the interest can frequently be deferred indefinitely. The policy loan will reduce the dollar value of the policy and, in case of death, the loan is repaid first and then the beneficiaries receive the remainder. Some older life insurance policies guarantee very favorable interest rates.

Assignment

This can be a source of low-cost funding for your business, but be careful that it doesn't short change your heirs and/or business partners should you die.

> **Epilogue**
>
> *In the event of your death, to protect your heirs and/or business partners, the situation can be covered by "key-person" insurance, which is specifically used for such purposes.*

39

Borrow Wisely

Borrowing money is one of the most common sources of funding for a small business, but obtaining a loan isn't always easy. Before you approach your banker for a loan, it is a good idea to understand as much as you can about the factors the bank will evaluate when they consider providing you with a loan.

The ability to repay must be justified in your loan package. Banks want to see two sources of repayment—cash flow from the business, plus a secondary source such as collateral. In order to analyze the cash flow of the business, the lender will review the business's past financial statements. Generally, banks feel most comfortable dealing with a business that has been in existence for a number of years because they have a financial track record. If the business has consistently made a profit, and that profit can cover the payment of additional debt, then it is likely that the loan will be approved.

Assignment

As stated previously, money is a commodity that is bought and sold and should always be treated as such. Keep this in mind.

If, however, the business has been operating marginally and now has a new opportunity to grow, or if that business is a start-up, then it is necessary to prepare a thorough loan package with detailed explanation addressing how the business will be able to repay the loan.

Epilogue

Money is one of the factors of production, but it is one of the more important and complex, requiring much review and analysis.

40

Equity Financing

Most small or growth-stage businesses use limited equity financing. As with debt financing, additional equity often comes from non-professional investors such as friends, relatives, employees, customers, or industry colleagues. However, the most common source of professional equity funding comes from venture capitalists. These are institutional risk-takers and may be groups of wealthy individuals, government-assisted sources, or major financial institutions. Most specialize in one or a few closely related industries.

Assignment

Equity funding is generally more costly than debt funding. You are giving up a stake in your business.

You may contact these investors directly, although they typically make their investments through referrals. The U.S. Small Business Administration (SBA) also licenses Small Business Investment Companies (SBICs) and Minority Enterprise Small Business Investment companies (MSBIs), which offer equity financing.

Epilogue

Do a cost/benefit analysis between debt and equity alternatives and select the one that is less costly and/or invasive to your business.

41

Uncle Fred Can Be a Pain

It is best not to borrow from friends and relatives, but many people do. If you must borrow from a friend or relative, do it on a business basis by putting the agreement in writing. Check with a lawyer if you want a binding legal agreement. You may also get a sample business loan contract form from a bank or lending institution. Use it as a basis for a written agreement both parties find acceptable.

Assignment

Be careful when borrowing from family and friends. Once they lend you money they will become your worse critics and will demand to stick their nose in your business on a constant basis.

51

> **Epilogue**
> *Unrealistic and/or naïve investment expectations have ruined many friendships and family relationships.*

42

Suppliers Can Be Lenders

Payment terms offered by your suppliers are a potential source of credit. Study the discounts for early payment and the penalty for late payment to determine the true cost of the credit. While some suppliers will extend credit only to well-established, proven firms, many will extend limited credit to new businesses to encourage another outlet for their merchandise. Planning for use of trade credit is essential. To establish good trade credit, a new business must make timely payments as agreed. Trade credit is effectively used by large businesses to buy products at lower cost than small firms. Do not depend too much on trade credit from one supplier. If repayment problems arise, you may find your major source for supplies cut off when you need it the most.

> **Assignment**
>
> Remember that net/30 means 30 days of borrowed money without paying interest. Try to get the best possible credit terms from your vendors. Many will tolerate a 60 day account without applying late fees or interest rates.

Epilogue

The difference between net/30 and net/60 is an additional 30 days of interest-free money.

43

Lenders Are Really Snake Oil Vendors

There are many sources for debt financing: banks, savings and loans, commercial finance companies, and the SBA are the most common. State and local governments have developed many programs in recent years to encourage the growth of small businesses in recognition of their positive effects on the economy. Family members, friends, and former associates are all potential sources, especially when capital requirements are smaller.

> ### *Assignment*
>
> There is more competition for small business loans than ever before. Shop around for the best rate and least restrictive loan covenants.

Traditionally, banks have been the major source of small-business funding. Their principal role has been as a short-term lender offering demand loans, seasonal lines of credit, and single-purpose loans for machinery and equipment. Banks generally have been reluctant to offer long-term loans to small firms. In addition to equity considerations, lenders commonly require the borrower's personal guarantees in case of default. This ensures that the borrower has a sufficient personal interest at stake to give paramount attention to the business. For most borrowers this is a burden, but also a necessity.

Epilogue
Don't be afraid to play hardball with lenders. Deep down they want to make that loan.

44

Not All Money Is the Same

There are two types of financing: equity and debt. When looking for money, you must consider your company's debt-to-equity ratio—the relation between dollars you've borrowed and dollars you've invested in your business. The more money owners have invested in their business, the easier it is to attract financing. If your firm has a high ratio of equity to debt, you should probably seek debt financing. However, if your company has a high proportion of debt to equity, experts advise that you should increase your ownership capital (equity investment) for additional funds. That way you

Assignment

Treat money like any other commodity. It's bought and sold for a price (interest rates) and should be treated as a "factor of production" in your business mix like any other business tool.

won't be over-leveraged to the point of jeopardizing your company's survival.

Epilogue

Be careful not to leverage yourself out of your own company.

45

Marketing or Bust

Marketing is based on the importance of customers to a business and has two important principles: All company policies and activities should be directed toward satisfying customer needs. Profitable sales volume is more important than maximum sales volume. To best use these principles, a small business should:

- Determine the needs of their customers through market research
- Analyze their competitive advantages to develop a market strategy
- Select specific markets to serve by target marketing
- Determine how to satisfy customer needs by identifying a market mix

Assignment

No product or service will succeed, no matter how good they may be, without understanding and executing a good and well-thought-out marketing campaign.

> **Epilogue**
>
> *Know your market. The customer is always king.*

46

Expand Upon Your Base

Key notions:

1. Always be on the lookout for new products or services. Seize those that offer promise. Only through product or service diversification can you lessen your risks in the marketplace, lower per unit cost, and enhance long-term profits.

2. Identify products or services that complement your existing lines. Sell these as supplements and watch your profits grow. For example, many small newsletter-publishing companies do not make money by selling the newsletter alone. The big bucks are generated by the sale of supplementary materials such as books and reports.

3. Become a primary source. Instead of distributing a product or service for someone else, investigate the possibility of primary generation. Develop the product or service yourself. You then

> **Assignment**
>
> Always be ready and open to modify every aspect of your product/service mix to better serve your markets and exploit new opportunities that may arise.

56

can control the product or service, sell to other middle-men, reduce your price, enhance your profits, and so on. In other words, you are in the driver's seat and not subject to the manipulations of vendors.

Epilogue

Maintain the flexibility to shift directions on a dime.

47

Judging the Markets

More than 50 percent of the profits that your business will earn five years from now will be generated from products or services that you are not now marketing, according to the U.S. Small Business Administration. Consequently, the question becomes: Are you able to absorb a 50-percent (or more) reduction in revenues? Probably not. So, don't make the mistake of assuming that the future will be a repeat of past performance and that profits will be forthcoming from existing customers and marketing practices.

Assignment

Judging markets is a roll of the dice, at best. You can minimize your risks by combining scientific research info with your gut instincts.

In an attempt to judge and exploit changes in customer behavior, various alternatives will become apparent. Don't take much time or invest a lot of money analyzing these alternatives unless you are sure there is a good probability of success. The name of the game is to locate various areas of business opportunities and to judge their commercial feasibility within a reasonable time frame and in a cost-effective manner.

Epilogue

Hire a professional if you need the help.

48

Give Them What They Want

Thinking that your product or service is the best thing to come down the pike since pantyhose is a common mistake made by many entrepreneurs. Keep in mind that it is only great if your customers think it is. Nothing else really matters.

Don't get me wrong here. Your opinions and the input of others, including experts, does have some relevance in the product/service selection process, but the most important thing is what the existing or prospective customers think. You can use the advice of others, or information generated through your own efforts, to manipulate consumer beliefs, but what ultimately matters in the buying process is what the customer is thinking and/or perceives.

The key to success in any business venture is the ability to predict what the customer will purchase. Even though buying habits can be manipulated by various stimuli, such as advertising campaigns, the best way to ensure profit fruition is to pinpoint your customer demands and future needs. Customer needs and desires can be identified by using formal surveys or by playing on hunches.

Assignment

Always remember that your "customer is king" and you give them the products and services they want, or convince them they need it. Your success is sure.

Epilogue

Always service your customers as if your next paycheck relies on it. It may.

49

Market Consideration

Before embarking upon a survey campaign you will need to identify your market. Few entrepreneurial endeavors have the capability of selling to everybody. Many are limited by the specialized nature of their products\services and\or geographic constraints. (Why sell snow tires in Miami?) In addition, lack of capital and marketing expertise could be factors that might restrict market penetration. At times, the market for a product or service is quite evident and

Assignment

Market segmentation is the wave of the future. Differentiate your product or service from your competitors along specific demographic lines to stand any chance of success.

rather general in nature. A drugstore would probably serve a specific localized customer base.

Market identification, sometimes referred to as "segmentation," is accomplished by studying "demographic profiles." In other words, all general markets can be segmented into smaller markets.

Epilogue

The old "shotgun" approach to marketing has gone the way of the rotary phone.

50

Competitive Consideration

At this point you know that you need to adequately identify the segmented market to which you want to sell. In addition, you must get to know your customers and determine how your product or service appeals to their needs and desires. As stated earlier, a survey campaign can help you accomplish this task. Now you must determine why your product/service will sell in the marketplace. Is it unique? Is it more economical than your competitor's? Does it have more attractive features or is it superior in quality?

One thing is sure, competitors cannot be ignored. To some extent, competition will determine the way you market your product or service and the price you ask for it. Ultimately, competitors will also determine the particular products or services you will market. To preserve your position against competitive pressures you will need to stay on guard at all times with the objective of outflanking your competitors. Your product or service must stand out from the

> ### Assignment
>
> You will always have competition. Don't fear it. Remember to keep your friends close and your enemies (competitors) closer. Watch your competition and learn from their mistakes and successes—even solicit advice from them.

others in the marketplace. Updating or modification of product or service lines may be needed periodically in order to beat the competition.

> ### Epilogue
>
> *You would be surprised how many of your competitors sing like a canary if you buy them lunch or a drink after work.*

51

Managing the Market Mix

Every marketing program contains four key components:

1. Products and Services. Product strategies may include concentrating on a narrow product line, developing

a highly specialized product or service, or providing a product-service package containing unusually high-quality service.

2. Promotion. Promotion strategies include advertising and direct customer interaction.

3. Price. The right price is crucial for maximizing total revenue. Generally, higher prices mean lower volume and vice-versa. However, small businesses can often command higher prices because of their personalized service.

Assignment

Identify and understand the sales components of the marketing mix, related to your products or services, and give those that are most important top priority within the overall mix, but don't forget the small stuff either.

4. Distribution. The manufacturer and wholesaler must decide how to distribute their products. Working through established distributors' or manufacturers' agents is generally easiest for small manufacturers.

Epilogue

Marketing is a mixture of sales techniques that achieves overall sales success.

52

Don't Forget Customer Needs

Customer needs and pref-
erential desires are influenced
by outside factors as well. Pre-
vailing opinions, media public-
ity and advertising, fads, and
trends can all manipulate demand for your products or services. The name of the game
is to pinpoint your market
and keep up on the factors
that cause your customers to
change their attitudes and tastes.

> ### Assignment
> Drive your business by
> the needs of your custom-
> ers or even create a cus-
> tomer need in some cases.

> ### Epilogue
> *Understand that customer needs are your market.*

53

Market Testing or Die

The real litmus test as to the worth of your products or services
is the marketplace's reaction to them. But before committing large

amounts of time and money to prove their marketability, you may want to conduct a test-marketing campaign. Simply put: it allows you to "test the waters" in a small way. This will give you the opportunity to assess the market potential of your wares. For example, a restaurant owner may want to supplement his/her menu even though the present food selection is adequate and profitable. Of course, the objective is to generate additional sales or to find new customers. Whatever the

Assignment

Test, test, and retest. It will save you lots of money and tears throughout the years.

case, before a menu modification is permanently adopted, the change should be tested for a short period of time to determine its acceptability to existing and new customers. If the change is not well received, a reversal can be executed without much difficulty or loss of time and money. The important point to remember here is that your customers must be aware of the efforts to implement change.

Epilogue

Don't jump in the water head first from a cliff. Look before you leap.

54

Marketing Data on the Cheap

When analyzing the marketing mix, most entrepreneurs quickly learn that there are two basic type of market research: "primary" and "secondary." *Primary* research is the collection of original data employing numerous methods including surveys, interviews, questionnaires, and so on. This method is generally too costly and time consuming for most small firms. *Secondary* data is simple information that already exists. Nowadays, it is easily accessible and dirt cheap to buy.

A good starting point is the *U.S. Industry and Trade Outlook*, published jointly by the U.S. Department of Commerce and the U.S. International Trade Administration. This is a goldmine of data providing an informational summary of every American industry. It covers the current state of an industry, the forces affecting that industry, and to where the industry is headed in terms of growth or decline. This work is available from McGraw-Hill. It is a little dated but still very useful with a new edition coming out soon.

Another good source is the *Statistical Abstract of the United States*. This work is the standard summary of statistics on the social, political, and economic condition of the U.S. Published by the U.S. Census Bureau every year since 1878, this popular resource is used by

---

Assignment

Check out the Websites related to the outlets referenced in Idea 54. They represent a treasure box of great information and assistance. Much of this information is free for the taking.

---

business leaders, academic institutions, libraries, marketers, planners, and researchers.

The Census Bureau has been compiling business information on every industry for the past 20 years and is a vast reservoir of informational resources. The U.S. Department of Commerce and International Trade Administration have data resources useful to all businesses doing market research.

The Commerce and Agriculture Departments in most state capitols can also be very useful, and, in some cases, more productive sources of information than the federal government.

Much of this information is free. Some will cost a little. It is well worth its price given the great expense inherent in the collection of primary data.

Epilogue

Don't turn down a free lunch. Free food (information, in this case) always tastes better.

55

Opportunities Galore

New products or services are your profit opportunities of the future, just as your current products or services generate today's revenues. All companies, both large and small, fall victim to the product\service life cycle. This underscores the need for your company to be constantly on the lookout for new opportunities. If you refuse to accept this business fact of life, your enterprise will not survive to see the future.

Assignment

Seize the moment, particularly when opportunity comes knocking. Give all potential opportunities a fair shakedown, but don't be so cautious that you talk yourself out of it.

Now, you must be consistently planning for the future in terms of new products or services. Even though there are risks involved in this process, it is a must in order to ensure the future of your entrepreneurial endeavors. You can look at it another way: new products or services will help your competitive posture in the marketplace and assist in future profit generation by replacing the old and less profitable lines.

Development of a new product or service should be given much consideration. After all, alot is at stake. In business, there are no guarantees of success, and hitting on the right idea by accident is usually the exception and not the norm.

Epilogue

After due consideration, your gut will tell you what to do.

56

Steps in the Marketing Research Process

The marketing process should be viewed as a scientific journey that is yet another important link in the business chain that ensures success.

1. Problem Identification. In this phase, the research problem is clearly defined. Questions that may need to be answered include, but are not limited to, the following:

   * Who are my customers?

   * Where are they located?

   * Why do they buy my product or service?

   * What will customers pay for my product or service?

   * How much/many will they buy?

   * How many times will they buy it?

   * Through what outlets will my customer purchase the product or service?

   * Who are my competitors?

   * What advertising media should be used?

   This list could go on forever. The questions that need to be answered ultimately depend on the product or service being marketed. Each will demand its own set of questions.

2. Initial Investigation. This phase attempts to put the research problem into clearer focus. Secondary (existing) sources of data are examined and experts in the field are queried for their opinions. Trade associations are primary depositories of helpful information.

3. Research Planning. At this point you know what facts must be unearthed. And you should be aware of how they will be obtained. Primary research (original surveys and forecasts) will be used interchangeably with secondary existing information in order to reach a decision.

4. Data Pursuit. Once the plan is delineated you can begin to collect the information. The choice of collection procedure depends on the plan and information available. It may entail telephone or mail surveys and e-mail contacts, as well as personal interviews.

5. Data Assimilation. After the data is collected, it must be interpreted and absorbed so as to assist in the decision-making function. This is also the phase where unscientific inputs, such as "hunches" and "gut feelings," may enter into the process.

Assignment

Apply these six "proven" steps in approaching market research. They are time tested techniques that you can use in all facets of your personal and business life in approaching problem resolution.

6. Conclusion. Once both scientific and nonscientific data have been interpreted, it is now possible to reach a conclusion. However, if the research process or the input data is flawed or insufficient, this reality must be reflected in the decision process.

Epilogue

Market research is like insurance. It helps protect against loss.

57

A Customer Relations Policy Is Money in the Bank

Dealing with customer relations can make or break your business. Your customers are your most important asset. Treat them as such. Have a standard policy in place to deal with problems that may arise with customers. Be sure your employees are well versed with that policy for they are often the "face" of your business in the eyes of your customers.

1.   Furnish your customers with a reasonable and easily understood guarantee of your services.

2.   If yours is a repair business, always return replaced parts to customers along with an explanation of what was wrong.

3.   If the bill is going to exceed your estimate, call the customer before you spend his or her money.

4.   Invest part of your time in training your employees in customer relations.

5.   Use follow-up letters and questionnaires to thank your customers and to determine if your service has been satisfactory. Use the information you generate to correct problems.

6.   Develop a code of ethics for your business. Put it in writing and communicate it to your

Assignment

Develop standard operating procedures (SOPs) for dealing with your customers and train your employees accordingly.

70

employees. Don't assume your employees know where you stand.

7. Make these policies known to your customers and tell them how they can reach you if they have a complaint.

8. Resolve complaints fairly and quickly. While you should "bend over backwards" to be fair, don't let yourself be victimized by consumer fraud.

Epilogue
Make your entire firm a "customer-driven" organization so your success will is assured.

58

The Customer Is King

An important factor that stands out very clearly when you are analyzing entrepreneurial success is the emphasis placed on "customer sensitivity." In fact, customer empathy is the one area in which small competitors can beat the big guys. Because of their bureaucratic nature, large firms are substantially displaced from their customers. Smaller enterprises, which can immediately identify with their customers, have the opportunity to empathize with their clientele quickly, which significantly

Assignment

Your best weapon against those who would raid your markets is customer service and goodwill, in particular, if the predator is a larger firm.

counters the competitive price difference used by the bigger firms. This factor explains why many small firms can successfully compete against large companies selling the same products or services.

Epilogue

Sincere one-on-one contact is still the best way to let people know you appreciate them.

59

Trial and Error

In reality, most entrepreneurs rely mostly on trial and error as a decision-making technique. Given that, as officially published by Dun & Bradstreet, approximately 60 percent of all entrepreneurial failures are due to an inadequate market for products and services. Relying solely on the trial-and-error method reminds me of the old Fram Oil Filter commercial on television. The message was clear—pay a little now or a whole lot later. The small investment input for a marketing survey and test program may more than offset the loss incurred due to a full-blown marketing campaign that failed. The trial-and-error method may be too costly in terms of losses incurred before rewards are achieved.

Assignment

Try to avoid "trial and error" as a business method in favor of more scientific approaches. It is generally cheaper over the long haul to take this path.

> **Epilogue**
> *Surveying and/or testing will not ensure success. On the contrary, there are no guarantees, but it does reduce the risk.*

60

Market Promotion and Strategy

So far, we have been dealing with the particulars of customer identification, buying motivations, competition, market testing, and feasibility analysis. Once you have determined that a market exists for your product or service, and that it can be exploited in a profitable manner, your next step is to delineate a marketing strategy.

It is beyond the scope of this book to examine the intricate details of marketing strategy. However, it is important for you to be informed of some broad concepts. I sincerely recommend that you seek out some marketing books at your nearest college library. Some of these works direct attention specifically to small-business marketing. Most tend to be more helpful than what is available in government publications.

> **Assignment**
>
> Do your homework. Market strategy and promotion is the "heart valve" that directs the efforts of the business to understand, identify, and exploit market opportunities.

> **Epilogue**
> *Marketing is the blood of your business, and promotions are the valves that keep it pumping.*

61

Controlling for Profits

You will always find successful managers looking over their shoulders. They utilize various methods that provide them with feedback data. This control information is used to help them manage more effectively. Now, this is where some entrepreneurs have difficulty. Many research studies have shown that some individuals who start their own businesses are not good managers. If these individuals do not rely on outside expertise or qualified employees, they're asking for trouble. Many go out of business or are forced to sell.

> ### *Assignment*
>
> Determine what good managerial skills you have and in which areas you are lacking. Plug the holes through education and/or professional help.

Just remember that a good manager will spot and solve a problem before it can threaten the enterprise. Procrastination is deadly.

> ### Epilogue
>
> *Search your soul for those skills necessary to make a profit. Whether it's pinching pennies to balance your check book, or seeking new markets, if you don't have the skills, someone else does and you should pay the fee for the expertise.*

62

Income Tax Is a Fact of Life

All businesses (except partnerships) must file an annual income tax return. Partnerships file an information return. The form you use depends on how your business is organized. The federal income tax is a pay-as-you-go tax. You must pay the tax as you earn or receive income during the year. An employee usually has income tax withheld from his or her pay.

> ### Assignment
>
> If you are generating profits, set aside an amount each week to pay your income tax when due.

> ### Epilogue
>
> *Filing and paying on time equals peace of mind.*

63

Estimated Tax

Generally, you must pay taxes on income, including self-employment tax, by making regular payments of estimated tax during the year, generally four times a year.

Self-employment tax (SE tax) is a Social Security and Medicare tax primarily for individuals who work for themselves. Your payments of SE tax contribute to your coverage under the Social Security system. Social Security coverage provides you with retirement benefits, disability benefits, survivor benefits, and hospital insurance (Medicare) benefits.

Assignment

Be sure you file your quarterly estimated tax form and pay what is due both to the federal and state governments, assuming your state requires the filing of estimated tax. Some do, some don't.

Epilogue

Be as accurate as possible in your estimates, as you can be severely fined for underpayment and non-filing.

64

Employment Taxes

When you have employees, you as the employer have certain employment tax responsibilities that you must pay and forms you must file. Employment taxes include the following:

- Social Security and Medicare taxes
- Federal income tax withholding
- Federal unemployment tax
- State income tax withholding
- State unemployment tax

> ### *Assignment*
>
> Don't borrow from this pot of gold as so many businesses do by not paying these taxes. The penalties and levy are very severe and can run as high as 48 percent a year.

Epilogue

File and pay these taxes on time. No questions.

65

Excise Tax

Here are the excise taxes you may have to consider:

- The manufacturing or selling of certain products, such as alcohol.
- The operation of certain kinds of businesses, such as trucking.
- The use of various kinds of equipment, facilities, or products.
- Receiving payment for certain services.

Assignment

List and pay those excise taxes on time. Sometimes considered "secondary taxes," they have a way of getting lost in the "pile" and then go unattended.

Epilogue

A tax is a tax, no matter how insignificant, that must be paid "sooner or later," and later means with penalties and interest.

66

Controlled Impulsing

Being impulsive has its obvious pluses and minuses. But if you know the "upside" of the behavior and can control the "downside," you are way ahead of most people and playing the game to win.

Many successful entrepreneurs are impulsive by nature, but they are not careless in that they will not allow impulsiveness to take a destructive path. Some argue that impulsiveness and quick-action-based gut instinct are one in the same. Actually, there are similarities between the two and they probably converge at times. Still others suggest that "boldness" is impulsive, if not well planned. General Patton was quoted as saying, "Boldness is the essence of strategy."

Impulsive actions and reactions are bad in and of themselves. Controlling the desire while imposing gut instinct and a little bold strategic thinking into the quick equation may pay dividends.

Assignment

Recognize impulsiveness for what it is: a long entrenched behavior pattern that materializes in the form of human desire. Understand it. Control it. Conquer it. And use it in concert with your other gifts to exploit your markets.

Epilogue

Impulsiveness can be fun when it manifests from some reason other than "I'm bored."

67

The Cash Flow Blues

You wouldn't believe how many entrepreneurs refuse to acknowledge the importance of financial information. Some of these people are operating on the notion that a checkbook is the only thing that you need in the way of financial statements. Many entrepreneurs are running $2- or $3-million-per-year enterprises shackled with the idea that rudimentary accounting systems are enough to do the job. I knew one gentleman who was running a business with four separate departments. He didn't know which departments were making or losing money. All funds were put into a soup bowl, so to speak, without being tagged to a particular department. Expenses were handled in the same manner. When this guy got into a cash flow bind, he had no financial feedback to work with when trying to remedy the situation.

The point to learn here is really simple: If you lack the appropriate accounting and financial expertise, go get some. Take some courses at your lo-

> ### *Assignment*
>
> Search for and find a reputable accountant who is experienced in all facets of small businesses. Additionally, read up on small-business accounting issues just enough so that you are not flying blind.

cal college or find some books discussing these topics and read them. The Small Business Administration also has some excellent publications concerning financial control and management. Write or call their headquarters in Washington, D.C., or the SBA field offices located in the state capitals. In addition, I suggest that you find an accounting firm that offers services in the form of providing monthly financial statements. This way you can have updated financial information on a regular basis. If difficulties crop up, at least you will know that trouble exists before much damage ensues. The charge is surprisingly inexpensive, normally ranging anywhere between $120 and $200 per month. This is truly a small sum when you consider the potential rewards in terms of financial control and containment.

What you have to watch at this point is the accounting firm. Make sure that they have experience with entrepreneurial enterprises. Ask around about their reputation. Don't ask for references, because they will give you their personal friends and most satisfied clients. Find out for yourself who they serve and then seek out those firms for comment.

Epilogue

"Help" is not a bad word.

68

Fall in Love With the Wastebasket

It's not a pleasant thought, but, at times, your trash can be a good management tool. Famed author and organization expert Barbara Hemphill put it plainly in her book, *Taming the Paper Tiger*, by suggesting "the art of waste basketry." In other words, immediately toss out the paper you don't need. Ask yourself these three questions:

1. What do I need to keep?
2. In what form do I need to keep it?
3. How long do I need to keep it?

Assignment

Go through your files and organize them by date, order of importance, alphabetically, or however best suits you and your business, and toss the unimportant or redundant ones.

Epilogue

Without a doubt, paper and documents can quickly accumulate and entirely consume you, creating a sense of personal and organizational paralysis.

69

High Pay-Off Actions

Now that we have traded off tasks for results, we must trade off results for results. Yes, there is a hierarchy of results. Some results are better than others. You must concentrate your activities and energies producing those results that will provide the maximum

Assignment

Quantify a results priority list and determine the importance of each by assigning a number in declining order of importance.

benefit to your business. Anything less, and you are cheating your business and yourself.

> **Epilogue**
> *Determine how much time and energy is needed for each priority and how each result can be achieved.*

70

Important Versus Urgent

Obviously, both the words *important* and *urgent* draw a serious note in most entrepreneurs, to be sure. You will find that many tasks are very important to you in achieving the desired results in your business. However, on occasion, the *urgent* need will strike, generally in the form of some business

> **Assignment**
> Determine which of your business activities are flexible enough to do without if an emergency arises.

crisis. You must have enough ingrained *flexibility* to set aside, on a temporary basis, even the most important tasks to your business to handle any crisis (urgent) situation that may arise.

> **Epilogue**
> *Make backup plans for your backup plans.*

71

Interruptions Galore

Many factors can affect your productivity as an owner/manger, but none more so than unwanted and unimportant interruptions. You will find that as your business grows, so does the number of questionable interruptions, in particular, those that deal with your employees. Telephone calls are a close second, followed by unwanted guests and friends who "just drop by" to say hello.

You must set standards in reference to these issues, or you will soon find yourself "consumed" and using an increasing amount of your valuable time engaged in unproductive endeavors. Your more productive side will cease to be a factor in the business, and eventually sales and profits will suffer as a result.

Assignment

Develop an internal radar detection system (gut instinct) and don't allow "time-takers" to steal your valuable time. They will if they can. Also, establish a protocol for taking phone calls and personal visits to your office.

Epilogue

Let it be known, in a friendly way, that proper protocol is law. You will find yourself with more productive time on your hands.

72

Results Versus Tasks

Many entrepreneurs are "task-oriented" to a fault. They forget that a "result" is more important than a "task." That is not to suggest that tasks in and of themselves are unimportant. Obviously, you must engage in tasks in order to achieve results. The trick is to maximize a particular set of tasks to achieve a result in the most optimum and efficient way.

Epilogue

Some people just keep doing "tasks" and achieving nothing in return. You know these types of people. They're a dime a dozen and just keep "chasing their tails" throughout life.

73

Technology Time Management

So far we have been speaking largely in terms of managing time and paper. Let us not forget that thing sitting on your desk and/or in your lap called a computer, much less the PalmPilot in your vest pocket, and even your cell phone. They are time management issues.

Don't forget: Proper data file management is just as important as managing your desk and paper trail. Keeping those computer files in organized folders, and your PalmPilot and cell phone storage links easily assessable and organized is very important to personal productivity and prudent time management.

Epilogue

Disorganization in these technical realms can be just as destructive to organization and personal effectiveness as pure paper issues.

74

Putting Your Finger on Time-Wasters

Effective management of your time is the key to ultimate entrepreneurial success. Whether you run a large or small company, one project or multiple projects at the same time, effective management of your time will help you stay focused and organized to complete the needed tasks in a cost effective matter.

You must understand the importance and challenges of effective time management, particularly in today's increasingly complex and competitive entrepreneurial marketplace. Improving your skills in terms of setting the correct priorities and identifying and eliminating time-wasting behavior will give

Assignment

Make a time chart (and be honest) about how you spend your time on the average workday.

you a better sense of "time" perspective and how it affects your operation. Hopefully, as a result, you and your company will both experience increased productivity, reduced stress, and most importantly, enhanced profitability.

Epilogue

Adjust the time chart according to some sort of organized and sane schedule that maximizes the efficient use of your time in accordance with your personal and business objectives.

87

75

Time-Wasters

Time is money, and the proper use of time is essential. Management consultant R. Alee MacKenzie has identified 15 time-wasters that can cost you in terms of lost productivity and profits. The list follows. As an entrepreneur, you must deal with them in an effective manner in order to ensure efficient operations.

1. Telephone interruptions.
2. Visitors dropping in without appointments.
3. Meetings, both scheduled and unscheduled.
4. Crisis situations for which no plans were provided.
5. Lack of objectives, priorities, and deadlines.
6. Cluttered desk and personal disorganization.
7. Involvement in routine and detail that should be delegated to others.
8. Attempting too much at once and underestimating the time it takes to do it all.
9. Failure to set up clear lines of responsibility and authority.
10. Inadequate, inaccurate, or delayed information from others.
11. Indecision and procrastination.

> ### *Assignment*
>
> Include these guidelines for interruptions and any other interruptions you can think of in a time management mix. Then act on it accordingly.

12. Lack of or unclear communication instruction.

13. Inability to say no.

14. Lack of standards and progress reports that enable a company manager to keep track of developments.

15. Fatigue.

Epilogue

As stated previously, the three leading time-wasters, according to MacKenzie, are telephone interruptions, unanticipated visitors, and meetings. Never forget them, lest they steal your very spirit over time if left unmanaged.

76

Prioritizing Time to Get Things Done

Here's what to do to maximize your "really" important time:

♦ Contract out tasks.

♦ Start with the most worrisome task.

♦ Complete deadline work early.

Assignment
Make sure you find time for yourself and your family.

♦ Know your capacity for stress.

♦ Stay organized.

- Take advantage of "down time."
- Get physical.
- Have fun.
- Divide up your time.
- Build flexibility into your schedule.

> **Epilogue**
>
> *What's the point of owning your business if you can't enjoy the most important profit of all: a good family relationship?*

77

Desire to Win

"Everyone loves a winner"—so goes the old cliché. Without a doubt, winning is contagious and a powerful motivator. However, the whole concept of "winning" must be put into proper perspective and analyzed.

Many entrepreneurs have reported that they have experienced one or more business failures before hitting the mark. Maybe of greater significance is the fact that research has shown that more than a few successful entrepreneurs were deprived as children. These early challenges gave them an incredible will to win. A. David Silver, the famous and well-respected venture capitalist, notes in his book, *The Entrepreneurial Life: How to Go for It and Get It* (John Wiley & Sons, 1983), that many successful entrepreneurs experienced a lack of social interaction and some educational arrest in their early years. Also, Silver explains that many were sickly in nature, had less wealth than their peers, and were small in physical build. In my own experience, I have noted that many entrepreneurs do, in fact, seem to be short and have small physical characteristics. Thomas J. Stanley, the author of the National Affluent Study, lends support to Silver's remarks by implying that successful people tend to have deprived childhoods. Stanley states, "…adversity is a better trainer and disciplinarian than anything else." Silver also credits some entrepreneurial successes to "achievement-oriented mothers" who press their offspring to succeed. Douglas MacArthur, who is now recognized as an entrepreneurial general, would have attested to this fact. I believe that all entrepreneurs who really want to succeed possess a "winning spark."

> ## Assignment
>
> Remember and learn from your hardships and frankly address your shortcomings and then find the spark that will thrust you into the realm of entrepreneurship. Write these items down and read them once a week. Burn them into your soul.

They can build upon past failures, misfortune, and personal flaws to reach great heights. Before becoming a mega-entrepreneur, media mogul Ted Turner took over his father's advertising business. The business was floundering and his dad committed suicide, yet Ted went on to build a thriving business. Our own late President Reagan was raised in a poor household dominated by an alcoholic father. His success speaks for itself.

Epilogue

Never forget where you come from or where you are going.

91

78

Letting It Rip

The proof is all right here, ladies and gentlemen. You can have all of the best ideas in the world, but if you don't convert those ideas into action, nothing will be accomplished. Even if your idea turns out to be something less than a winning one, at least you experimented with that particular approach and the results can be recorded for future reference. So, take the initiative and direct your creative energies into tangible, innovative results. Just remember the words of Jack Paar, who said, "Life is a series of obstacles, and we ourselves are the largest obstacles." Don't fall prey to cancerous inaction. If you are willing to experiment and learn, your ability to successfully convert ideas to innovation will increase.

Assignment

When you create your business plan, focus on adaptability, advancement, enhancement, replacement, and expansion options for the future. And don't let grass grow under your feet unless you want your competition to steal your turf.

Keep in mind that your survival in the present and future entrepreneurial environment will depend on your ability and willingness to apply new ideas in a changing marketplace. Many small companies are reporting that they are diversifying their product and service lines in order to stay afloat. Products and services come and go. You must keep abreast of your market and know when to change. Without ideas in hand ready to go, you may miss the boat. Even if the market for your products or services is growing, you still may have to engage in creative and innovative endeavors to thrive. Why is this the case? Because we find ourselves in a highly competitive economy in which everybody and his brother is trying to start a business. Attraction of future customers will depend on your success in standing apart from your competitors. In other words, doing something different, will help you in the game of entrepreneurship.

Epilogue

"If you snooze, you lose."

79

Motivate Yourself to Success

There is no set formula that guarantees to stimulate your entrepreneurial motivation. In Idea 77, some widely held beliefs about why people seek out entrepreneurship were discussed. Obviously, a healthy and constructive dislike for your employer definitely provides a push. Likewise, other factors influence the decision to take the plunge. Whatever the case, you have to decide what motivates you the most and then play on

Assignment

Find that "burning passion" and play it like a fiddle until the titillation dives you to move forward.

those stimulii. Visualize where you want to be in five or 10 years and keep those objectives before you consistently.

93

Epilogue

Just remember, "The only thing to it is to do it."

80

Taking the Bull by the Horns

It's not enough to identify changes in your market and select local opportunities. You must be prepared to quickly pounce on the prey in a profitable manner. Here is where we separate the men from the boys. Through the years, I have seen dozens of entrepreneurs fail to act on apparently profitable opportunities for many reasons that cannot be adequately explained within the confines of this book. However, one reason stands out predominantly, and that is the "fear of failure."

Assignment

Create a risk/benefit-assessment plan to help decision-making in order to seize new opportunities when they are presented.

Now, I do not advise that you jump at every opportunity for the sake of dealing with your fears, but the constant unwillingness to make a decision even after completing a proper investigation of an opportunity is paramount to laying the foundation of entrepreneurial demise. At some point you have to take the bull by the horns.

Epilogue

Convince yourself that not trying is worse than failure.

94

81

Capital

All businesses must be concerned that an adequate amount of capital is available to begin and support operations. Service firms, by their very nature, are generally less capital intensive than other types of businesses. Therefore, they can operate on the proverbial shoestring.

Assignment

Money is the blood that makes the business work. Manage it accordingly.

Epilogue

Keep enough in the bank for emergencies—a blood bank, so to speak.

82

Channels of Distribution Are Key

Most manufacturers must worry about getting their products in the hands of the ultimate consumer. In many cases, this is accomplished through the use of intermediaries, which are commonly referred to as "middlemen." These intermediaries are links in a channel of distribution and help move the product to its destination.

Wholesalers must also be concerned with this matter because many employ middlemen known as agents and brokers to facilitate the flow of their products to retailers. Service businesses should not be overly concerned with channels of distribution because most services are performed by the originator. Some businesses franchise their operations to achieve growth. In these cases, the franchisee would serve as the distributor for the franchisor.

The following is a list of the more-common channels of distribution:

Assignment

Getting your product/ service to the end user is like navigating a river. You must have a planned destination, a way of getting there, and sound tools for getting there. In other words: Know where you are going, know your winds and currents, and make sure your ship is sound. Check the rudder.

- ◆ Manufacturer-Wholesaler-Retailer-Customer
- ◆ Manufacturer-Broker-Wholesaler-Retailer-Customer
- ◆ Manufacturer-Broker-Agent-Wholesaler-Retailer-Customer
- ◆ Manufacturer-Broker-Jobber-Wholesaler-Retailer-Customer
- ◆ Manufacturer-Broker-Retailer-Customer
- ◆ Manufacturer-Jobber-Retailer-Customer
- ◆ Service Originator-Customer
- ◆ Service Originator-Agent-Customer

Many products and industries have standardized channels of distribution that have been used for years. Some companies mistakenly think they can reduce costs and increase profits by eliminating middlemen. Most firms that attempt to do this fail in their efforts. Always remember that intermediaries are specialists in their fields and they know the ropes. Consequently, they are cost effective to use even though they charge commissions and represent an added link in the channel.

Epilogue

Distribution cannels are like rivers. Sometimes they're smooth, sometimes they're choppy, but they're always moving and filled with hidden holes, so watch out.

83

Beware of Global Warming

Some manufacturing and retailing establishments must consider the effects of climatic conditions on their business. Failure to do so could be detrimental to profitable operations. For example, some years ago the Del Monte Corporation built a large pineapple cannery in Mexico on a river. The fruit groves were located up-river. During picking season the fruit was to be barged down-river to the cannery for processing and shipment. Management failed to consider one very important point and it was a costly mistake. The river's flood stage and picking season happened at the same time. Consequently, the river could not support barge movement and the factory was never used. Millions were lost due to failure in considering the climate's effect on operations.

Retail firms can also be affected by climate. Stores and shops located along coastal resorts can be adversely affected if unseasonably cold weather grips their areas for a season or two. Likewise, retail businesses in winter resorts can experience the same fate if a warmer than normal winter occurs.

Wholesaling and servicing enterprises are not affected by weather as compared to the aforementioned establishments. Wholesalers sell to retailers and, therefore, it is the retailers' responsibility to get the products to the ultimate customers. Service firms normally take the product directly to the customer, thereby minimizing the impact of weather on a potential customer. For example, an electrician or plumber will work rain or shine. Of course, extreme weather conditions can stymie any operation.

Assignment

Climate can affect your business. Nowadays you better plan for "rapid climate change" and the effects it will have on your business. Then, prepare and adjust your business strategy accordingly.

Epilogue

You may have to move south.

84

Competitors Are Really Sharks

Assignment

When in the big fish tank called business, you can't avoid the sharks at all times. Just don't feed them and make them your friends.

The impact of competition is important to any business operation. The degree and strength of competitive forces within a particular market should be considered and evaluated very carefully to determine the effects on existing or prospective endeavors. Is there room for another seller? If the market is crowded with competitors, can an enterprise with exceptional management skills survive or prosper, forcing other less-efficient firms to concede market share?

Epilogue

Make strategic alliances with some competitors to muscle out others.

85

Credit Policies Are a Must

Most businesses are forced to give customers credit privileges because of competitive forces within markets. A standardized credit policy is a must in order to establish uniformity and minimize the possibility of credit discrimination. In addition, it will establish procedures for granting credit and collecting past-due accounts.

Assignment

There is such a things as "firing your customer." Those who don't pay or pay very slow are not worth the bother in most cases. Set up a credit system that works for your business.

Epilogue
Collect your money in a timely manner or you will find yourself getting roasted by your competitors.

86

Delivery as a Business Process

Product delivery is a primary concern for wholesale and manufacturing operations. These organizations must deliver their products to the appropriate link in the channel of distribution in order to ultimately sell the goods. Some retail firms, such as mail-order companies, are also involved in the process of delivery, although to a much lesser extent than the previously mentioned types of businesses. Service companies normally do not worry about delivery because services are delivered when performed; however, here are exceptions. For example, consulting firms, research firms, photocopy centers, and so on, may be involved in the delivery of various papers and reports.

Epilogue

Timely deliveries are money in the bank.

87

Economic Climate, Not the Weather

The systematic risk inherent in the overall economy will affect all businesses. Having an idea when recessions will occur can help ensure proper preparation and thus defend against the impact of economic downturns. It is interesting to note the number of companies who fail to take heed of a recession's warning signals and fall victim. Businesses that are on guard usually weather the storm, and some even prosper.

The more common recession signals are:

- Steady increase in the general level of interest rates. (When short-term rates exceed long-term rates it is called an "inversion" and a recession will generally follow suit.)

- Falling economic output.

- Falling corporate profits.

- Leading economic indicators constantly down.

Assignment

Stay on top of business and financial news. Read the business section of your newspaper and watch CNBC, a great source of business news.

- Consumer and business confidence constantly negative.

- Consistently rising levels of business inventories.

Epilogue

I know someone who states that he makes money by watching the news. He buys and sells stocks on trends that are reported on in the nightly news.

88

Financial Control or Die

Maintaining financial control of a business is contingent upon managing resources to generate adequate profit levels. The management of physical, financial, and intangible assets would fall in this category, and are discussed throughout this book.

Assignment

A business without financial control is like a ship without a rudder. You will wander and hit bottom, or maybe rocks.

Epilogue

It's like saying prayers every night. Know thy numbers.

89

Government Regulation Is Costly

Local, state, and federal government regulations affect all businesses, both large and small, costing the American business community approximately $750 billion per year. Even though the larger firms tend to be watched more closely, small firms are expected to abide by all codes and statutes. Writing to government agencies and requesting information on laws affecting a particular line of business would be wise.

Assignment

Government red tape is only getting worse each day. Figure its cost into your price structure.

Epilogue

Uncle Sam doesn't accept ignorance as an excuse. Learn what you need to know about the government regulations that affect your business.

90

Industry Trends Are Important

Assignment

You must stay on top of what's going on in your industry or risk falling behind and losing market share. With technology changing things so rapidly, this is more true today than even before.

All businesses must be concerned with events taking place within their industries. Even though the overall economy is recovering from the recession, many industries are failing to respond. Some will never regain their former strength and a few will slowly die. The service industries have, for the most part, been unaffected by economic downturns. In fact, services that now account for 75 percent of the nation's output will climb to 80 percent of economic activity by 2010.

Checking activities within a particular industry will help gain insight into the dynamic forces working to strengthen, stagnate, or weaken performance in that area.

Epilogue

They say that taxes and death are the only guarantees in life, but change should be added to that list.

91

Inflation Risks Are Real

Inflation affects all businesses. Initially, the results of rising inflation are quite positive, with sales and profits increasing, although much of the increase is artificial. For example, if a business achieves a 10 percent return on investment (ROI) one year, and inflation for that same period runs at 8 percent, the firm has only realized a 2 percent gain on its investment (although most companies would report a 10-percent increase). Many establishments actually base expansion plans on

Assignment

History has shown inflation to be one of the five major causes of empire collapse. Truth be told, deflation is far worse. By historic standards inflation is low. It peaked out its ugly head recently and tucked back hurriedly when the government raised its sword (interest rates) to fight it back. Look for inflation to remain low for some years to come.

inflated figures and later down the pike experience a capital squeeze because (inflation adjusted) accounting records were not used to make the decision.

All financial and accounting records should reflect the damage caused by inflation. Failure to do so could lead to disaster. In addition, high levels of inflation (exceeding 10 percent per year) generally cause recessions. So inflation can be viewed as an indicator of future economic vitality. Conversely, lower levels of inflation (2 to 4 percent) are considered good for the economy. An economic system experiencing either no inflation or deflation (declining price levels) is thought to be in serious trouble, like Japan was a few years back.

Epilogue
Be conservative in your adjustments and always adjust your figures for inflation.

92

International Events Cannot Be Avoided

The United States has joined the world economic community out of necessity because of resource dependency. Consequently, the American economy is subject to forces beyond the immediate control of domestic leaders. Some lines of businesses are more affected than others. A knowledge of international forces that may do harm to particular industries and firms will help to ensure survivability if negative events occur.

Much has been said about the inability of American manufacturers to compete with the more efficient and productive foreign counterparts. This is largely true, and domestic producers will have to respond in order to survive. On the other hand, retailers and wholesalers may be affected only temporarily due to overseas competition, because they can always change to more marketable foreign products. Service firms are generally insulated from foreign competition because most nations haven't concentrated on exporting services as of this date. In fact, the service sector is considered an area where American firms could compete successfully in the international marketplace, though outsourcing has become a problem as of late.

Assignment

We are still the only "super-power" on Earth, but we're fast losing our ability to control al events. American gross domestic product as compared to the rest of the world has declined, which will affect our abilities to project power. Therefore, events far outside our borders, and thus out of our leaders' control, will be affecting your business more and more.

Epilogue

China will replace the United States as the world's largest economy in 15 or 20 years from now.

93

Labor Is Expensive

All firms must ensure that adequate human resources are available to support operations. A manufacturing firm should be concerned that a particular location has enough skilled, semi-skilled, and managerial talent. Businesses offering technical services may be interested in the number of qualified technical personnel who could be hired in a given location.

Assignment

Labor is a factor of production that you need. Manage it wisely. It is the most costly resource that you will employ in your business.

Epilogue

Firms failing to consider the implications of an inadequate labor supply before starting or relocating operations will suffer the additional cost of attracting needed individuals located outside the immediate area of operation.

94

Licensing Is Necessary

Most local and state agencies require business establishments to apply for any number of licenses. In addition, many want payment of a flat and/or percentage of estimated sales fee before granting permits. Requirements vary from one area to another. Larger concerns may need federal permits. For example, a license must be acquired from the U.S. Department of Commerce before a firm may engage in export activities.

Assignment

Small firms should check with the local clerk of the Court. They will have information concerning any local, state, or federal licensing requirements for particular types of businesses.

Epilogue

The bureaucrats want their share, and it's getting worse as local and state cash-starved governments attempt to use licensing as a way to raise money. They will continue to think of new "licensing scams" to get money and, unfortunately, we entrepreneurs must always pay.

109

95

Market Research Must Be Done

Market research is necessary to determine whether a product or service can be successfully sold. This research, if conducted properly, will reveal the threats in the marketplace as well as any opportunities that may exist. Many small businesses fail because they do not consider the impact of competitive forces and overestimate the customer base. Market research will address these weaknesses.

Assignment

Market research is your best insurance against failure in the marketplace. You don't have to over do it and spend a lot of dough.

Epilogue

Much market research has already been done (called secondary research) and can be purchased inexpensively online or through government agencies.

96

An Operations Policy Helps Manage

An operations policy explains the procedures to follow in maintaining effective operations. Generally, the need for operations policy increases as a firm grows. It is not surprising to find many small retail or service businesses operating efficiently without an operations policy.

Assignment

SOPs are a must if you don't want to go crazy. It relieves you of the stresses and difficulties associated with micromanagement.

The standard operations policy should include a description of key functions within the business and who is in charge of each. An organizational chart would normally be part of the policy manual, along with a description of responsibilities and spans of control to reduce administrative overlap. Standard operating procedures (SOPs) would be established for each function.

Epilogue

A statement relating to events not covered by SOPs is generally incorporated with policy to reduce confusion if an exceptional situation were to occur. Some call it crisis management.

111

97

Pricing for Success

All businesses must worry about pricing their products and services. After all, the prices chosen will affect a firm's ability to successfully compete. Price setting can be a complicated task. Many things need to be considered carefully. For example, if the product/service is new, a higher price can normally be set. Conversely, strong competitive forces within the market would force a lower price. Pricing strategy should also be integrated with long-term goals. A "skimming" price policy means that a firm is setting a high price in order to achieve large profit margins. However, a lower market share is achieved. Consequently, when competitors enter the field, the ability to survive will be in question due to a thin customer base. On the other hand, a "penetration" policy sets a lower price to achieve wider market acceptance, which helps to fight off competitive threats.

Assignment

If you can't sell your products or services and cover your expenses while making an adequate profit, stop in your tracks. Many businesses have gone belly-up by generating unprofitable sales.

Epilogue

No matter how "married" you are to a particular product or service, if you can't make money, walk away.

98

Product/Service Will Dictate Success

The product or service offered will determine business success. Obviously, many products and services are widely available today from many different sources. Some will continue to be in demand while others will stagnate or die. New ones will come and go. The trick is to find a line that has achieved some degree of success in the marketplace with a lot of growth potential and only a few competitors.

Assignment

Remember, all products and services go through a business life cycle. Some will go away forever, some will stick around in a mature state not generating many sales, and others will make a market comeback.

Franchising is attractive, but a franchise is only as good as the product or service it represents.

Keep in mind that changing economic conditions could alter what constitutes a positive or negative proposition.

Epilogue

The business life cycle is like taxes, death, and change: It's always there to be dealt with (in some form), and it doesn't go away.

99

Raw Materials Are Important for Some

The location of raw materials is of primary concern to manufacturing outfits. Some will locate their operations near sources of raw materials in order to minimize the cost of transportation that is usually passed on to the manufacturer. This is usually the case where raw materials are extremely heavy and bulky. For example, many steel mills will locate near coal mines. In addition, availability is a major consideration. Manufacturers must ensure that adequate raw materials and/or components are available to keep production flowing. Failure to deliver finished goods to customers on time may result in a loss of goodwill.

Assignment

If you are dependent on raw materials to produce, you had better be sure you are located near supplies and/or have access to them.

Some manufacturers may attempt to optimize their location between major customers and sources of materials needed for production. In some cases, it may be more advantageous to locate near markets as opposed to suppliers. It could be that both market and raw material locations are minimized in favor of a location that is more favorable because of wages, taxes, and/or climate.

Epilogue

Have a back-up game plan, in case a key supplier folds or moves away, or something else, such as a natural disaster, affects your supply.

100

Research and Development Is an Investment

Research and development is a primary concern for manufacturing firms for several reasons. Without the new products or processes initially created through research-and-development efforts, a company's ability to compete effectively would be compromised. In fact, many economists feel that the U.S. manufacturers are becoming less competitive than foreign firms because industry as a whole is spending much less on R&D (inflation adjusted) than it did a decade ago. At the same

Assignment

The term R&D means many things to different people. Even the small firm must engage in R&D, on some level, in order to survive. It doesn't have to be a big investment or major deal within the business, but even being on the lookout for new products or services to sell is a form of R&D.

time, foreign manufacturers have been increasing their R&D emphasis. This situation underscores the necessity of maintaining an adequate R&D program if the future is to be met with success.

Retail, wholesale, and service businesses should concern themselves with research and development to the extent that trends affect their marketing endeavors. Obviously, existing products and services will give way to new ones. The trick is to know when these events will happen and how they can be exploited.

Epilogue

Research will help you keep your product/service mix relevant in a changing world.

101

State of Technology and Your Business

Technology is changing the way all firms conduct themselves in the marketplace. Failure to acknowledge and use the latest in technical innovations will lead to demise. To illustrate, many American manufacturers have failed to innovate to the same degree as their foreign competitors. Consequently, international markets have been

Assignment

Determine which emerging technologies will affect existing and/or prospective lines of products or services, and to what degree. Outline how these changes may be exploited profitably.

losing to the more productive foreign producers. Even on a smaller scale, those retailers and service firms failing to consider the impact of technology on their existing lines will fall victim to changing demand patterns.

Epilogue

Don't fall behind, lest your more technical competitors will eat you alive.

102

Storage Is Important

Assignment

There are such things as too much storage or too little. Either is costly when you expend more than is needed or you lose customers because you do not have product on hand. Try to "optimize" the exact space you need.

A retail business must store inventory in order to fulfill customer wants when immediate demand occurs. Some retail outlets succeed or fail based on their ability to provide a quick and adequate supply of their product, especially in a competitive market. Wholesalers and manufacturers generally need larger storage facilities to accommodate the enormous volume of finished and unfinished material that must be stored until production or shipment is made.

Storage is not a big problem for service firms, because services are intangibles and cannot be warehoused.

117

Epilogue

The right amount of storage space is important. Too little might cause production and delivery delays, thereby resulting in a loss of customer goodwill. On the other hand, underutilized space is wasteful and is not an expense covered by revenues.

103

Topography May Limit Your Options

Many areas are not conducive to manufacturing facilities because of land contour. There is one county in the state of Virginia in which 85 percent of the land has an incline exceeding 15 degrees, which is considered restrictive for manufacturing and large wholesaling purposes. Normally, this situation would not affect retail or service establishments, which tend to be smaller by nature, although any area that is largely inaccessible would be bad for businesses dependent on traffic flow. Another thing to be considered is the impact of no industrial growth.

Assignment

Generally, this is most important in manufacturing and distribution businesses. The general rule of thumb is that an incline of more than 15 degrees can create expensive problems.

Opportunities for any type of business may be restricted if overall growth is stymied. To illustrate, the seat of the aforementioned county

118

is a town of 8,000 people. It has one of the highest failure rates for small businesses in the state. Main Street is littered with empty storefronts and many existing operations are barely afloat.

Epilogue

"Location, location, location" is not just a mantra for real estate. It is a necessity in business.

104

Trade Credit as a Managing Tool

It is wise to check with prospective suppliers about their credit arrangements. If the business is new, it can expect to pay cash on delivery for merchandise and supplies during the first few months of operation. This obstacle can be overcome if the owner has a good credit rating and is willing to personally guarantee payment. Then immediate credit terms are normally available.

Many businesses do not pursue better terms with a supplier after a relationship has been established. One small motorcycle and repair shop in Virginia was dealing with four different suppliers for 18 months and all were demanding cash on delivery. A consultant advised the owners to write and demand favorable credit terms or other vendors would be found. Three graciously gave credit while one refused. Luckily, the one that resisted was the smallest and least important of the four.

In addition, ask suppliers for a discount upon making early payments. Many will grant a 1 or 2 percent reduction for paying bills within 10 days. Evaluate the cost of paying cash, taking into consideration the discount against the advantage of using the float (suppliers' credit). The answer will be determined by analyzing the rate of

Assignment

Trade credit is a source of interest-free money that must be managed properly. Don't abuse it, because you will be cut off by your vendors. Then it's COD, and that can hurt you financially.

return on utilized dollars. For example, if the average annual rate of return on invested capital exceeds the annual adjusted rate of the suppliers' discount, it would not be wise to make early payments because the business can make more return by using the suppliers' float. If the rate is less, early payments may be appropriate.

Also, playing one supplier against the other for purposes of securing better credit terms might be a good idea at times. Many businesses have found that some vendors will extend payment terms from the traditional net 30 days to 45 or 60 days. In some industries, terms of 90 to 180 days have been achieved.

Epilogue
Keep the vendors happy. Cash up front is a deathblow to many businesses.

105

Vendors Are Not Your Friends

Most small retailers purchase from wholesalers who, in turn, buy from manufacturers and/or jobbers. Manufacturing firms must buy their raw materials and components from other sources. It is important to remember that all businesses should have several sources of supplies readily available. Relying on a single vendor can be risky. What happens if the vendor goes out of business or changes marketing approaches, deciding not to include particular types of businesses?

> **Assignment**
>
> Don't rely on a single source and negotiate the best terms. Play your vendors against one another. Don't feel guilty about it either.

> **Epilogue**
>
> *It may be wise to let suppliers know that several vendors are being used. It will keep them on their toes. It may be useful to play them against each other to negotiate better prices.*

106

Vendors May Squeal

> **Assignment**
>
> Ask your vendors about the industry you are servicing. Some will sing like birds, others may be somewhat reserved, but the few who talk are be valuable sources of information.

Some vendors provide a wealth of information and help to new or existing businesses in the field they serve. A few suppliers will even go so far as to set up an entrepreneur in business by providing location, inventory, and financial assistance. Most do not go to those extremes, but many will help in one or more of these vital areas.

Constantly search for new suppliers. Evaluate their services and credit terms carefully. It is not unethical to play them against each other. In fact, it makes good business sense. Tell one or more suppliers that a better deal can be obtained elsewhere. Watch for their reactions. Some will bend and others will not.

Epilogue

"Ask and ye shall receive"—maybe. But it doesn't hurt to ask.

107

War on Margins

Depending on what you are selling, your vendors can make or break you in a hurry. Don't let the nice demeanor and smiling face of a sales representative draw you into a false sense of security. It's a war out there in the commercial arenas with "profit margins" at stake. It is a constant tug-of-war between you and your vendors, and who captures the most "margin" for the dollar spent.

If you are buying products using the Internet, such as hardware tools, in some cases, the prices you pay for the same quality product can vary as much as 30 percent, depending on the wholesaler, sub-wholesaler, or jobber.

Even when you buy services to run your business, it pays to shop around extensively. I have never noticed much difference between OfficeMax and Staples in terms of pricing, but both are good sources. Both run item by item special sales on occasion. Buying your office supplies from a discount catalog supply house can produce additional savings of up to 65 percent. The same can be said of your printing needs in reference to business stationery.

One area in which you need to shop very carefully is insurance. Insurance rates for the same coverage provided by highly rated mainline insurance companies can vary as much as 50 percent. I have found that it pays to go directly to insurance companies that maintain their own sales forces or exclusive agents. They tend to be much cheaper. However, most of these are "cookie-cutter" programs. If your business calls for a unique insurance package, an independent agent may be your only choice because they specialize in many different kinds of insurance and represent several different insurance firms at the same time.

Assignment

List vendors you generally trust and the ones you know you can squeeze for additional margin. Play one against the other. Use this group of vendors exclusively; unless a better deal comes walking through the door from a trustworthy source.

The most important thing to remember is that, if you pay too much for a product or service, your profit margin is going to suffer. It's money left on the table that spills into some else's pocket.

Epilogue

It truly is a war of "margins" with distinct winners and losers. Just remember, vendors aren't your friends, they are smiling "pickpockets."

108

Warranties Are Real Promises

For competitive reasons, most businesses must give warranties that guarantee the successful performance of their products or services. Warranties, whether implied or expressed, are contracts that must be taken seriously. Broken warranties can lead to costly legal battles with disenfranchised customers, not to mention government agencies. In addition, the possibility of bad press must be taken into account, and the loss of goodwill it will cause. When considering warranties, try to estimate the cost of making such guarantees and what means will be used to deliver what is promised.

> ### Assignment
>
> Nowadays in this competitive environment, guarantees are a must. Keep your promises because, if you don't, it will get around within your industry and you will gain a nasty reputation and your goodwill will begin to disappear.

When projecting warranties, try to do it in a novel and unique way. A new slant can do wonders to stimulate sales. For example, a couple of years ago a mail-order firm decided to incorporate a unique approach to making a guarantee. The company in question told potential buyers that their checks or money orders would not be cashed for 30 days and, if they were not satisfied with the product, it could be returned within a month. Upon the return of the merchandise, the uncashed monies would be sent back. The favorable result of this new twist was tremendous.

Epilogue

Never lie to your customers, and always deliver what you promise.

109

Road Map to Success

A business plan has been traditionally viewed as a document used in raising capital to start or expand a business endeavor. How-ever, it does have another pur-pose that is largely ignored. The business plan is first and fore-most a "planning" device. Its secondary function is to raise capital. The preparation of the plan forces you to entirely evalu-ate the prospects for success or failure in the marketplace. Cre-ation of a good business plan is a grueling process taking months to complete. The final plan,

Assignment

Constructing a business plan is a must. It's your road map to success. It doesn't have to be a 500-page book—30 to 100 pages will do.

ranging anywhere between 30 and 100 pages in length, is the ulti-mate testimony as to whether your product or service will be suc-cessful in the marketplace. The process forces you to look at everything related to the business venture beginning at the present and extending five years into the future. Capital requirements, com-

Constructing a business plan is like taking out an insurance policy, it will minimize your risks. Whether you are just starting your entrepreneurial enterprise or are already in operation, it is essential to develop a business plan. In the process, both opportunities and hazards will be identified. The plan may convince you not to pursue your venture further; in this case, it has done you a favor. Why throw money down a hole? On the other hand, the business plan could verify the need for a particular product or service, but at the same time it may force you to change your attitude toward distribution, marketing, warehousing, and so on.

Epilogue

Remember, a business plan is, first and foremost, a "planning" document and, secondary, a document used to raise money.

110

Are You a Good Decision-Maker?

Decisions, decisions, decisions. It seems like every time we turn around, we have to make more decisions. The question is, "Are you a good decision-maker?" If you aren't (or don't think you are), there is no need to worry. Decision-making is a skill that can be learned by anyone. Although some people may find this particular skill easier than others, everyone applies a similar process.

There are two basic kinds of decisions:

1. Those that are arrived at using a specific process.
2. Those that just happen.

petition, and operational consid-erations are but few things re-viewed and dissected in the business plan.

Although both kinds of de-cisions contain opportunities and learning experiences, there are definite advantages to using a specific process to make a de-cision. The most obvious advan-tage is the reduced level of stress you will experience.

Wise decisions are made us-ing a definite process. They are based on the values and percep-tions of the decision-maker and include carefully considered alter-natives and options along with periodic reassessments of the decision and its effects.

Assignment

Create a set of guide-lines for decision making sometimes called SOPs (standard operating proce-dures), but leave enough decision flexibility for spur of the moment issues that may arise and are not covered under the SOPs.

Epilogue

Wise decisions may or may not follow societal norms and expectations, but they are right for the decision-maker based on what they know at that point in time about their options. In other words, don't let conformity drive decisions.

127

111

Common Decision-Making Mistakes

As much as we would like to believe that we do not have any prejudices or biases, it is a fact that everyone does. The more aware you are of yours, the better off you will be. The main reason everyone has their own way of viewing the world is because our brains simply cannot take in everything, at least not on a conscious level.

Have you ever tried to learn 10 new things all at once? If you have, you know that it is very easy to become overwhelmed and end up learning very little at all. That is because of the way the brain works. Our brains screen and categorize information so that we can understand the world around us without being overwhelmed by it. We get into trouble when we fail to realize that many of the perceptions we hold are based on what society (parents, teachers, the church, all institutions, and so on) teach us, not what we actually know to be true.

Assignment

There is no such thing as a perfect decision-maker. But there good ones, bad ones, inbetween ones, and then those who make no decision out of fear or because of their inability to do so. Assess which is you and plug the holes if possible.

The following is a list of the most common decision-making mistakes. By learning about these pitfalls now, you will be able to avoid them in the future:

- Relying too much on expert information.
- Overestimating the value of information received from others.
- Underestimating the value of information received from others.
- Only hearing what you want to hear or seeing what you want to see.
- Not listening to your feelings or gut reactions.

Epilogue

You may have to invest in some other people to complement for your own weaknesses.

112

Excellence Pays Dividends

Enough has been said about excellence to last a century, but listen just one more time.

Consumers are becoming increasingly quality-conscious once again. They are unimpressed by the cheap alternative that is second-rate and produced in a slipshod way. Many companies, both large and small, are taking the hint. You should also apply some quality control standards to your product or service. Constant improvement is necessary in order to stay ahead of the competition nowadays. You may be thinking that because your enterprise is a small operation, a quality control program is not affordable in terms of money and\or time. However, even a simple program can

129

Assignment

Always strive for excellence in your business endeavors. Your customers, vendors, and bankers will take notice. Positive results will always follow a business approach based on excellence and professionalism.

produce tremendous feedback in terms of improvement suggestions. In other words, ask your customers for input and ideas.

Also, you will need to impress upon your employees the need to excel. If given the right combination of reason and incentive, your employees will go out of their way to make you and the customers happy in terms of quality and service.

John W. Gardner, former secretary of the U.S. Department of Health, Education, and Welfare said, "An excellent plumber is infinitely more admirable than an incompetent philosopher. The society which scorns excellence in plumbing because plumbing is a humble activity, and tolerates shoddiness in philosophy because it is an exalted activity, will have neither good plumbing nor good philosophy. Neither its pipes nor its theories will hold water."

Epilogue

The strive for excellence always pays off in the end.

113

We Be Metric

General George Patton once said, "Boldness is the essence of strategy." Any small firm wanting to jump into the international marketing arena is taking a bold step. So, how can you tell you are ready?

Do you know how many feet are in 100 meters? Or do you know how many centimeters equal an inch? Because 80 percent of global businesses use the metric system, you better brush up on your "new" math.

There are really no set guideposts. International competition, saturated markets here in the United States, and expanding global consumerism are creating challenging opportunities and reasons for moving in the international direction.

However, you must "look before they leap," in particular when it comes to tapping markets far from home base. Importing is less demanding in terms of due diligence, but none the less, requires ongoing investigation.

More potential customers will demand that you quote in their currency and communicate in their home language. To date, it has been very difficult for American businesses to accept these new realities as recent news accounts have reported.

Brush up on your Spanish and French. Spanish is the number-two language of commerce and French is considered the global diplomatic language. Take some cultural studies courses.

The good news is that the federal government provides a bonanza of useful information and direct assistance to help domestic entrepreneurs wanting to pursue international business, in particular, exporting.

Assignment

Take the plunge in international business, but do some research and homework and don't throw caution to the wind. Also, be prepared to understand and conform to the way people do business in other countries.

Through its International Trade Administration (ITA), the U.S. Department of Commerce's direct assistance is the granddaddy. The U.S. Small Business Administration's Office of International Trade is also a source of assistance, as is the U.S. Department of Agriculture for agricultural products and services. These agencies are now cooperating with each other to help integrate the American business community into international trade. They all have Websites, so do the Google thing.

Some state government assistance programs match or exceed the level of assistance provided by the federal government. Call the Department of Commerce within your particular state and ask for the international trade desk.

The private sector is also awash with helpful resources. Import/export management companies, commission sales agents, and custom house brokers, will act as your international sales department and absorb the burden of international trading (for a fee of course—usually 5 to 10 percent of gross sales). The ITA can help you find these firms.

Foreign and domestic state Chambers of Commerce are generally helpful, and many large banks have international trading departments that provide a wealth of useful information and advice, if not direct assistance.

Small firms can operate just as smoothly and profitably as larger companies nowadays. A small $3-million-a-year manufactureer of steam boilers in Frederick County, Virginia, is successfully selling its products in China. If they can sell steam boilers in the tough Chinese market, there is truly an international market for any American product or service.

Epilogue

Know the market and its needs before you take the plunge. Remember: Eskimos don't need icemakers.

114

Managing Cash and Credit

Always remember that money is a commodity that is bought and sold for a price (interest rates). It is one of the most precious resources available to a business and requires effective management if the firm is to survive and prosper.

Send out invoices consistently and promptly at about the same time each month. The bills should contain all relevant information about the sale (date purchased, cost, account balance, terms, and so on). When income is received from receivables or cash sales, deposit it promptly in interest-bearing checking accounts or other insured accounts that can be drawn on readily. After paying obligations due, put the remaining cash back into the operation immediately so as to generate additional sales and profits. Idle cash or money sitting in low-yielding accounts is not an example of effective money management

Be sure that accounts receivable are current, and take steps to keep them that way. Past-dues can be costly if money must be borrowed or existing funds used to finance operations until accounts are collected. Therefore, credit and collection control procedures are critical to successful operation. Grant credit based upon certain conditions that may vary depending on the customer. This can be accomplished by evaluating potential accounts relative to their ability to pay. After that, payment terms and credit limits can be established. Also, existing accounts should be reviewed periodically in order to determine if changes in credit arrangements are necessary.

All prospective and existing accounts must be required to fill out a credit application form. The form should include a promise to pay according to the terms of the credit agreement and it can be used to investigate customers' credit history. Be sure the application has a release statement allowing permission to conduct a credit investigation.

If accounts are offered to customers, expect some problems to surface, especially during periods of economic recession. Normally, it is advisable to work with slow payers instead of being overly rigid and perhaps losing business as a result. Set up procedures for dealing with slow or delinquent accounts. Degrees of slowness should be established with the objective of applying increasing measures of pressure the longer the overdue account remains unpaid. Extreme cases may have to be pursued legally. Many of these delinquent situations can be avoided if standards are developed and instituted to disallow existing or prospective customers from billing beyond their ability to pay.

Assignment

Collect your money as if there is no tomorrow and never pay your bills late, unless you have a good reason not to. If that is the case, always communicate with your creditors in an honest and open fashion.

When the business decides to use credit, always exercise conservatism and precedence. Pay bills on or before due dates so as to maintain a healthy credit history. A bad payment record can be expensive when losing credit privileges and incurring higher interest charges from worried lenders. Take advantage of early payment discounts if they are economically favorable from a cash float standpoint (savings generated from the payment discount must be greater than the income that could be created by using the money in another way, before the invoice is due).

In addition, maintaining good relations with all creditors (including bankers), can prove to be beneficial in the long run. Keep them informed as to what is happening with the business.

Here are some tips that may help to accomplish this information function:

- ◆ Be candid about positive and negative situations. Many creditors will work with a business in a difficult environment if they are aware of the problems besetting the enterprise and its industry.
- ◆ Help the creditors to understand the business and industry. Sometimes ignorance is the biggest stumbling block to effective relationships.
- ◆ Provide some insight into management and control functions. This will gain the creditor's confidence and faith as it shows a willingness to make things operate smoothly and efficiently.
- ◆ Be specific about short-term, intermediate-term, long-term, and crisis planning. Creditors dislike unanticipated disruptions. Tell them when things are going to take place.

It is not necessary to incorporate the previous tips into creditor relationships, but they will help relieve some of the natural and obvious tensions that exist between borrowers and creditors. An atmosphere of mutual trust and respect will also be fostered, leading to a lasting and growing relationship.

Collect your money as if there is no tomorrow, and never pay your bills late, unless you have a good reason to. If that is the case, always communicate with your creditors in an honest and open fashion.

> ### Epilogue
>
> *It may take more time and effort to collect on a bad debt then what it's worth, but you don't want to send out the image that you're a pushover to customers and suppliers.*

115

Managing Growth the Right Way

Growing too fast can be as hazardous as a no-growth situation, if not more so. Growth must be implemented and managed carefully to ensure that the business does not expand beyond its ability to control and/or finance operation. Many firms have met with demise because of uncontrollable expansion. The giant W.T. Grant failed because it grew beyond its capability to finance expansion internally and externally. The result was bankruptcy.

Growth should be mapped out well in advance. Within

> ### Assignment
>
> Growth can kill your business if not controlled or managed properly. Your growth objections should be incorporated into your business plan.

these plans a reasonable estimation of resources necessary to carrying out objectives must be evaluated and scrutinized to determine the feasibility of expansion. If resources will be lacking because of internal constraints and/or external factors, expansion objectives should be altered to meet with the realities of the situation.

Epilogue

Keep focused on your growth goals, and look for growth opportunities, but don't overshoot the mark.

116

Never Say Never

Several weeks ago, I came across an Associated Press article concerning the television series *Star Trek*. The article went on to quote the creator, Gene Roddenberry, as saying, "When *Star Trek* was first shown on television, it was so unpopular that my own father watched it, went out, walked up and down the street and apologized to all the neighbors." Of course, the network stuck it out and the rest is history. Also, in the world of entertainment, we have the late country music queen Patsy Cline. She came from humble beginnings and lived on the wrong side of the tracks in Winchester, Virginia. In the late 1940s and 1950s she resided on Kent Street, an area of Winchester that had a large concentration of blacks and poor whites. She had a beautiful voice and would sing in any tavern that would give her a booking. She was outspoken and at times ran with some questionable people. This led to people of Winchester (a small, conservative, and quiet town) to reject and even disown her in some ways. Even today, many people in Winchester scorn her and there are those who refuse to go along with the renaming of a street in her honor. This jealousy is unbecoming a community that, at one point in its history, elected George Washington to his first public office. Pasty never gave up and always thought in big terms. It was this drive that took her to Nashville, where she found success and fame. Patsy was also responsible for the discovery of another great country music talent: Loretta Lynn.

In their earlier careers, many of our presidents suffered humiliating defeats and crushing blows only to bounce back stronger than ever. This better prepared them to meet and overcome the challenges that lay before them. In fact, the difficult early years built a strong foundation that supported their efforts to achieving the highest office in the land.

Assignment

First, you need an objective. Write it down. Second, you must visualize the objective and see yourself accomplishing it. Third, keep on pushing, trying, investigating, and experimenting until you hit upon the right combination that will unlock the realm of entrepreneurship.

Epilogue

It may take years and several tries, but in the final analysis you will find that your greatest ally was persistence.

117

Organize Yourself

Once you have identified your goals and have your "plans of action" in place, the next step is to organize the factors of production (land, labor, capital, and management). These factors make it possible to offer something, a product or service, to sell. They are interrelated. In other words, all four must exist simultaneously, or conducting business would not be possible. This does not mean that each of the factors carry the same weight of importance. To the

> ### *Assignment*
>
> The organizing function is where you separate the men from the boys and the women from the girls. It's the point at which you must commit your financial resources.

contrary, each factor will carry a different degree of importance depending on the particular situation. For example, firms that are equipment- and\or labor-intensive will demand large working capital requirements. On the other hand, service enterprises are generally small by nature, and the primary initial emphasis is placed on management.

Epilogue

Organization and focus go hand in hand.

118

Set Your Goals Now

Not only do you need to have identifiable goals and objectives, but a plan of action is a definite must. Very few individuals have become successful entrepreneurs without knowing where they are going and how they are going to get there. If you are still working for somebody else, set a timetable for breaking away and taking the plunge. However, if you are currently an entrepreneur but lack goals and specific plans, now is the time to sit down and do some thinking.

The following is a list of some common goals that you may consider. Please be advised that this is not a complete list by any stretch of the imagination; they are offered as a guide only. Great care should be taken when delineating one's own goals. Every individual situation is different and necessitates careful consideration and unique planning.

- I want to be self-employed within the next 18 months.
- I would like to provide for all of my family's needs within two years.
- I want to be financially independent within 10 years of starting my own business.
- I would like to employ my wife and/or children.
- I would like to pass on a viable business to my heirs.

Your goals should be so constructed that there stands a reasonable chance of attainment. Goals that are unrealistic will only lead to frustration and non-fulfillment. In addition, keep them simple and to the point.

Assignment

If you don't set personal goals and goals related to your business, you're a ship without rudder, and you are going to run aground.

Once your goals have been visualized, the next step is to formulate various plans of action that will provide you with a road map into the realm of entrepreneurship. "Action plans," as we will call them, are multipurpose guides that will point you in the right directions.

Epilogue

Make sure your plans are reviewed and evaluated as time progresses, and modify if needed.

119

Short-Term Suicide

Don't fall prey to your impulsive desires and aspirations. There are already too many people in this country chasing get-rich-quick schemes and the like. The slipshod and second-rate reign supreme today, largely due to quick market decisions and a less than adequate commitment to quality and the long term. These individuals, given the increasingly charged competitive environment, will not survive to see tomorrow.

Whether you are already in business or are a prospective entrepreneur, just keep in mind that jumping from one idea, product, or service to another will generally lead to failure and frustration. You need to concentrate and focus your energies on specific and stable objectives. Of course, there are individuals who can spot trends and take advantage of them quickly. They have the ability to get in and out with amazing speed. Now, most of us do not possess this quality. In this re-

> **Assignment**
>
> Make sure your short-term goals fit into and lead to your long-term goals.

gard, it would be wise to investigate opportunities thoroughly and then persist when it makes good sense. However, always keep alert as to changes in the marketplace and be prepared to alter your plans as the environment dictates. Oftentimes, guarded flexibility, with long-term objectives always in mind, is a better alternative than "turning on a dime." Moving too quickly presents the danger of overreaction and miscalculation.

> **Epilogue**
> *Coordination of goals is very important to small business survival.*

120

Sweat Buys Equity

You are about to read the most important section of this book. It deals with the subject of "persistence" as it relates to entrepreneurship. When conducting the research for this book, I asked what factors lead to entrepreneurial success. Seventy percent of those queried stated or implied that persistence and perseverance were the most important elements.

The following list is a selection of some quotes from a few of the entrepreneurs researched:

- "I attribute my success to a lot of hard work and determination."
- "Dedication to hard work."
- "Persistence."
- "Drive."
- "Stick-to-it-iveness and never giving up."
- "Perseverance."
- "Perseverance and hard work."
- "Long hours and hard work."
- "Hard work."
- "Patience and perseverance."
- "Being thoroughly dedicated."

Experts in the field of entrepreneurship are sure about one thing: The more you persist, the greater your chances of succeeding at entrepreneurial endeavors are. There is another thing to consider here: If you sell your business at some point in the future, you will find that there is generally a direct relationship between price and longevity. A longer life will attract a higher price.

Assignment

Success is 99 percent perspiration and only 1 percent luck. Never give up or let up. "Endeavor to Persevere" as the old Indian Chief said in the movie *The Outlaw Josey Wales.*

143

"Staying the course" can pay dividends, as the late great President Reagan often said. And he should have known, being one who fought for his program and beliefs without giving in to much compromise. Reagan, like other entrepreneurs who persist, reaped the rewards of steadfast planning, confidence, and unparalleled faith in his decisions.

Epilogue

"Anything worth doing isn't easy." It's an old cliché by an unkown author, but its good reason.

121

10 Steps to Wise Decision-Making

This process can be applied to any situation in which you need to make an important decision. If you follow these 10 basic steps, you will find yourself making wiser decisions in your professional as well as your personal life.

1. Define, as specifically as possible, what decision needs to be made.
2. Write down as many alternatives as you can.
3. Think about where you could find more information about possible alternatives.
4. Check out your alternatives.
5. Sort through all of your alternatives.
6. Visualize the outcomes of each alternative.
7. Do a reality check. Which of your remaining alternatives are most likely to happen?

144

8. Which alternative fits you? Review your remaining alternatives and decide which ones feel most comfortable to you.

9. Get started! Once you have made your decision, get moving on it. Worrying or second-guessing yourself will only cause grief.

10. How is it going? Be sure to review your decision at specified points along the road. Are the outcomes what you expected?

Assignment

You are not born with decision-making skills; they are acquired as a result of your life experiences, education, and surroundings. That's good news because it is a "learned" process and that means you can acquire the skills necessary to plug the gaps in your decision-making abilities.

Epilogue
Hire someone who can help you if you don't have the expertise needed for good decision-making.

122

Truth or Consequences

Once operations commence, there is a need to utilize control through the use of feedback procedures. Productivity, sales, profit, and quality-control reports are but a few of the feedback mechanisms that can be employed to determine whether you are doing things right. It is not enough to just sit back and watch your entrepreneurial enterprise operate. An intricate part of management entails controlling, through feedback, to ensure effective operations. You may have the best product or service in the world, but to rely on that alone isn't enough. The sales of this product or service may not be generating sufficient profits, or imperfections may be too high.

Assignment

Feedback is the oil that lubes the wheels of progress in business. A feedback system can be as simple as an employee "suggestion box," which is a good start, all the way to complex customer and vender satisfaction surveys. These systems are tools used to correct problems within your business that may be adding to inefficiencies and thus having a negative impact on the bottom line.

Epilogue

Continued and appropriate feedback control will inform you quickly of difficulties before large-scale damage is incurred.

123

Technology Assessment Planning

Create a master plan for technology, just as you would draw up a business plan, a budget, or a marketing plan. Design the plan so that it supports your business strategy and goals. Use it to guide technology buying decisions. Think of technology purchases as investments, not costs. And, remember, when you have an overall plan, your company avoids wasting money on unnecessary purchases or quick fixes.

Start by determining your company's needs. Look at what problems need to be solved and how technology can help. Get expert help to guide you. Check your *Yellow Pages* under "Computers-System Designers and Consultants," or ask your local Chamber of Commerce. As always, get references.

Many factors that affect your business are tied to a technology cycle. To ensure that

> ### *Assignment*
>
> Changing technical conditions, both internal and external to your business, will force you to update and modify your business plan at least once a year. Twice a year is better.

your technology plan continues to serve you well, make it a habit to update it annually. Set aside a block of time near the beginning of the calendar year, fiscal year, or whenever is most convenient for you to update.

147

> **Epilogue**
> *Technology is like a knuckle ball. It weaves in and out of your business, so beware.*

124

Technology Is a Must

Any business that is worth starting must have the right technological capital. Of course, the most important piece of technology you're going to need is a computer. The work to be done determines what type of machine you need. If you just need a simple record-keeping machine, you can get a bare bones machine for a few hundred or less. If your work involves architecture or graphic-intensive work, then you will need a workhorse. Internet connectivity is a must in this day and age and you should get the best connection speed and performance that your business can comfortably afford.

Keeping up with technology is just another burden on you as an entrepreneur. Maximizing its usage and minimizing its costs will definitely increase your firm's bottom line.

In reference to your computer hardware and software system, you have undoubtedly been faced with using a "pre-packaged" (canned) system verses a "custom" designed system. If all you truly need is an office machine, then, by all means, go with the Dell or Gateway deal of the week, but if you need more power and capability, then go custom.

Assignment

We live in a technical world where technology leaps are occurring very rapidly. Don't be left behind, because you won't survive. Assess the technical environment of your industry and do what is necessary to maintain your position in the marketplace via your competitors.

Yes, it will cost you a little more to go custom in reference to hardware, but at least you will get a system built to the exact needs and specifications of your business. Also, servicing your system will be a lot easier given that local hardware vendors usually service what they sell.

As far as software is concerned, the price of developing custom software is just too cost-prohibitive nowadays for most small firms with software developers earning an average of $100 per hour. In addition, the prepackaged, canned stuff on the market today (in particular in reference to accounting software) is hard to beat for the price.

There may come a point in your business life at which customized software makes sense and you can afford it. Generally, the bigger and more complex a business becomes, the more the need to customize software.

Epilogue

Don't let technology eat your lunch. Manage it properly like any other business challenge you face.

125

Websites Are a Must Nowadays

Obtaining, maintaining, and marketing a Website for your business is relatively easy to do. The actual design of the site should be done professionally so as to promote your firm's professionalism. As with everything else in your small business, however, you should be involved in all aspects of its creation and operation. The first thing your site needs is its own URL or address on the Web. *GoDaddy.com* or *NetSolutions.com* can register the domain name for your site for a small fee and reserve it until you're ready to open the site to the public. Next you need a Web-hosting service. *Valueweb.com* and *ipowerweb.com* both offer plenty of space and tools for designing the site, including e-mail accounts, file-transfer capability, even streaming audio and video to really put your message out there. Of course, the most well-designed and user-friendly site in the world is of no help to you if customers can't find it. So, the next step is to register your site with Google and Yahoo. They allow you to put any relative terms to your business into their search engine so, when a customer is looking for something relating to the words you entered, your site is listed for

> ### Assignment
>
> A good Website design isn't enough. You must market. There are many good small Web-design companies out there in every community. Seek their advice. Most are also affiliated with people who can market your Website as well.

them. If you actually pay them to list the site, it gets listed toward the top of the results, giving you a more prominent place in the customers' options of sites to check out. All of these are relatively cheap ways to set up shop in cyberspace, costing small monthly or yearly fees.

Epilogue

Yahoo and Google have great marketing tools, and can also assist you in building your Website.

126

Always Compare

Assignment

Feedback control is necessary to ensure adequate profits. Comparing results and estimates should be done no less than monthly to spot trouble areas and then move quickly to correct it.

Compare your expected results against your actual results. Because your business plan sets forth marketing, operational, and financial milestones, you should carefully analyze actual operating results against the goals and objectives established in your plan.

Epilogue

You're probably sick of hearing this by now, but study your numbers constantly. Sales, expenses, growth, decline— learn to love looking at the data if you want to survive.

151

127

Tweak It to Death

Parts of your business plan may feel very tight and others still may need some work. Look for ways to improve upon what you've done so far. Incorporate the experience you've gained as a business owner into your business plan. Anticipate future events—good and bad—that may affect your business.

> ### *Assignment*
> The tighter the better. Make it short, concise, sweet, and easy to ready, and change if necessary.

> ### Epilogue
> *Take appropriate action if goals outlined in your plan haven't been met.*

128

Update Your Plan

Your business plan is a working document that will work *for you* if you use it to remind yourself and your team where you are going and how you will get there. Whether you're updating your business plan for the first time or the 20th, treating your business plan as a dynamic document that evolves through time will prove to yourself and to others that you understand your business and you know what is required to make it grow and prosper.

> ### *Assignment*
> Again, the business plan is first and foremost a planning/guiding document—a road map to success.

> ### Epilogue
> *Be sure your accountant, and maybe your attorney if you operate in a highly regulated industry, sees and approves changes to your plan.*

129

Cheerleaders Wanted

Build a team of supporters for your business—friends, family members, and colleagues who routinely talk up your business to their friends and acquaintances. Make sure that they know enough about your qualifications and capabilities to make an accurate and convincing case to others.

> ### *Assignment*
> Give your team the ammunition you need to "make your case" and "tell your story."

Epilogue

Selling yourself is just as important as selling your product or service.

130

Play the Game

Get involved with professional associations related to your industry or field. You'll get to know experts and colleagues in your specific market. And they may know of immediate or potential opportunities for your business. Other good networking opportunities include local or regional business associations, Chambers of Commerce, and nonprofits aligned within your field.

Assignment

Networking within the right circles can produce great results in terms of finding new clients. Local Chamber of Commerce mixers and state Chamber of Commerce events are prime pools.

Epilogue

Many private "network" clubs do monthly meetings for the same purpose. Ask around about these.

131

A Thank You Goes a Long Way

At the conclusion of all successful projects, thank your customers for their support and express your interest in working with them again. Also, encourage them to pass along your name to others. If your operating budget can handle it, consider offering discounts for customer referrals.

Assignment

Capitalize on your customer goodwill and ask them for referrals. This is a big source of new business for many small firms.

Epilogue

Don't forget your employees in the customer relationship business. Ultimately, it's your employees who make a lasting impression with your customers. Once again, your employees are the "face" of your business.

132

Bragging Rights

Take advantage of opportunities to show what you know by offering free presentations or articles on timely issues to business, professional, and community organizations and publications. Make sure that your presentation/article is relevant to listeners' interests, not a thinly veiled commercial for your business.

Assignment

Many newsletters work wonders, as do speeches to local and regional civic organizations. Get the word out.

Epilogue

Be sure your presentation is topical. Nothing turns off people faster than superfluous and unnecessary information.

133

Make That Call

Don't wait for customers to call you. Contact them from time to time to see how things are going, personally and professionally; what issues or trends they deal with; and perhaps alert them to an event, article, or Website that may interest them. Also, consider issuing a newsletter to current and prospective clients with relevant news, tips, and other information that can help their business, or simply brighten their days.

Assignment

Keep in touch with your clients on a frequent basis. Don't be annoying with three telephones calls a week, but subtle reminders that you are around are perfect.

Epilogue
This shouldn't need stating, but don't beg for customers or sound desperate when you call.

134

It's Nice to Have Friends

Every small business should have a network of colleagues and associates to call upon to handle excess workload, or provide service or experience you may not have. These relationships almost always result in "reciprocal referrals" to you.

Assignment

Form an "advisory board." You don't have to meet, but ask them to be available one-on-one or collectively by phone if you need them in a pintch or just to talk over any business matter.

157

> **Epilogue**
> *Take your "advisory board" out to lunch and pick up the tab. It's cheap advice.*

135

Kiss the Booty

There's no better source for a positive referral than a happy customer. And remember that the quality of your service says as much about you as the quality of your work or product does. Responsiveness, the ability to help out with tight deadlines, and a willingness to do those all-important "little things" (for example, working in small jobs for no charge) builds goodwill and a good reputation for your business.

Assignment

Remember, customers are your bloodline. Do what you can to make them happy—at all costs. If sometimes goes wrong, be upfront, call or visit with them, keep them in the loop, and never lie. And do it better the next time around.

> **Epilogue**
> *Humility buys a lot of leeway and goodwill.*

136

Become an Idea Generator in Three Easy Steps

Close your eyes, kick up your feet, sip a glass of wine, puff that cigar, take a ride in the country, go hunting, do yoga and so on—but whatever your fancy, let your mind run wild while you're at it. These are but a few of the many processes that can generate idea output:

> ### *Assignment*
> There is a good reason the turtle beat the hare. Be patient and allow your new ideas time to grow roots.

- Germination. Allow any new ideas the chance to germinate. Unless you're in a crisis situation, it is better to sit on an idea for a little while.

- Idea expansion. Once a creative idea has been accepted by the mental process, it is not unusual for the idea to build upon itself and therefore enhance your opportunities.

- Evaluation. Once an idea or group of ideas is accepted as a solution to a problem, it should be tested.

Epilogue
Constantly brainstorm new ideas for products and services, or just how to do things better within your business.

159

137

Creative Thinking Techniques

Creative thinking is like riding the waves on Venice Beach or having your back to the wind in a tall ship at sea; it opens up your perceptions that allow you to break the bonds of traditional thinking that, at times, traps us all.

1. Be open to new ideas. In order to be creative you must be positive and keep an open mind to new ideas that may initially seem impractical, but after careful consideration, take on pragmatic characteristics.

2. Problem empathy. You must be able to identify problems that threaten your entrepreneurial endeavors. In fact, problem identification is the most important step in the decision-making process. Unfortunately, this is the point at which most entrepreneurs fail the test of good management—recognizing problems and acting to solve them. Remember the old adage, "A good manager is one who solves a problem before it becomes a problem." In other words, the problem is neutralized or minimized before it threatens profits.

3. Prep yourself. Be prepared to immerse yourself in ways to defeat a problem. This process will include the collecting of detailed information and the delineation of proposed a course of action.

4. Initate ideas. In this stage, you attempt to generate as many new

> ### *Assignment*
>
> Aim at the heart of the business problem as a marksman on the rifle range and then employ your natural and learned talents to solve the problem.

160

ideas as possible. A greater number of ideas will increase the probability of finding a viable solution. If
you have other associates, you may want to engage
in a "brainstorming" session.

Epilogue

*Creative thinking is easy. Just sit back, relax, have a glass
of wine, and let your mind run wild. You will be surprised at
your mental output.*

138

Calculating the Risk Factor

Assignment

Approach risk with an
open mind. Analyze any deal
or business decision very
carefully, but don't over do
it. Many people over analyze
and talk themselves out of a
good deal or it's just an excuse because they are re-
ally "weenies" at heart.

It is known from research
studies that successful entrepreneurs are "moderate" risk-
takers. They are not the "dice
rollers" that many purport them
to be. The Center for Entrepreneurial Management (CEM)
found that of the 2,500 entrepreneurs responding to their research, 40 percent would take
3-to-1 odds at a racetrack, 15
percent would try 2-to-1 odds,
while 23 percent would opt for
a 10-to-1 shot. Twenty-two

percent indicated they would go for the daily double and a chance of making a bundle.

If you are an acute risk-taker and in any way have "gambling fever," don't take the entrepreneurial plunge, because you will probably lose your shirt. Even if you are a moderate risk-taker, caution is still needed. You must analyze all deals in terms of risk versus reward before making a decision.

Epilogue

Taking a reasonable risk is a matter of proper calculation.

139

Go for It

Today, we find ourselves in trying economic times and circumstances. Fluctuating interest rates, inflation, increasing oil prices, and conflicting tax reforms all seem to be converging at the same time to produce a very challenging entrepreneurial environment. Times may never be more precarious.

Assignment

If you are prepared and have done your homework, "there is nothing to it but to do it."

If you want to take the plunge, and you feel ready, by all means do it now. Five years may bring a different set of economic directions that may or may not be advantageous to small business activity, but you can be sure that if you wait until the perfect time, it will never come.

> **Epilogue**
>
> *Remember the words of the Greek philosopher Sophocles, "Heaven never helps the man who will not act."*

140

New Ideas Are Money in the Bank

Business, nowadays, breeds from new ideas. It's the modern fuel that keeps every business moving and "breeder" working on new products, services, ideas, and methods.

1. Scrutinize any new idea to the maximum degree. Don't leave any stone unturned. This provides peace of mind.

2. Determine and record all of the negative and positive aspects of any new idea. What benefits can be expected in terms of improved marketing, lower costs, enhanced productivity, and so on? Who will receive them? Are there any risks associated with implementing the new idea? If so, what are the risks? Can a mistake be absorbed? Good managers always visualize the worst-case scenario and then make a determination as to whether they can survive that possibility. If they think not, a new idea will be forthcoming.

3. Once the idea has been analyzed for possible flaws, restructure it so that the idea is simple to understand

and interpret. This will help you to clear your thinking about the new idea.

4. Review your idea with other people who may have already utilized a similar approach. Customers, competitors, consultants, accountants, and other experts could provide input. Idea weaknesses must be candidly admitted and addressed. The idea may need to be modified or even eliminated in favor of a new approach.

5. Execute the idea at the proper time. Wrong timing may cancel out the benefits of a good idea. For example, trying to execute productivity improvements by using new techniques could result in a morale backlash unless employees have been properly prepared for the introduction of new methods. This orientation might take several weeks or months.

> **Assignment**
>
> You must clip away at your ideas until they take form and thus provide usefulness to your business.

6. Evaluate the results of implementing your idea. Without proper feedback, you may never know whether an idea is working until a lot of damage has been inflicted. In addition, you can monitor your batting average.

Epilogue

Ideas are like stones: lifeless and of no meaningful shape until they are put into motion.

141

Never Say You're Sorry

If you have tried your hand at entrepreneurship and failed, you have nothing to feel sorry about. Even if you never attempt to take the plunge again, at some time in the future when you're sitting around the fireplace with your grandchildren on your lap, you can always tell them that you made a stab at being your own boss, unlike most people who never took the risk.

This brings to mind my father. He was a failed entrepreneur who tried his hand at wildcat coal mining, produce retailing, and beer distribution. Upon being asked about his entrepreneurial failures several weeks before his death, due to acute and prolonged heart illness, he said, "I have tried what many will never attempt to do. When I leave this world, don't feel sorry for me, because my life has been full."

> **Assignment**
>
> When you're 75, don't tell boring stories to your grandkids around the fireplace. Even if you have failed many times over, at least you tried.

Epilogue

You never have your "day in the sun" hiding under a rock.

165

142

Developing Ideas

Many good ideas come and go quickly. They are lost to the moment and are never recovered. You should prepare yourself when you have that "idea flush."

1. Always record your ideas. Any thought can become fleeting in a hurry. Write it down or record it.

2. Lay back and let your mind run wild. Often the best time for idea generation is when you're relaxed or doing something enjoyable. Take 20 or 30 minutes a day and set it aside for creative thinking.

3. Always look around and question. Never take anything at face value, especially in the world of business. Poke, pry, and question everything. Question the motives and the actions of your competitors, customers, employees, suppliers, and, yes, even yourself.

4. Build upon and expand the base of old ideas. The implementation of old ideas can lead to the creation of a new one. Keep in mind that many new ideas are just refinements of past ideas. Carefully evaluate old ideas with the intention of extracting new approaches.

5. An existing idea can be modified to yield a new one. Changing an idea (either adding to or subtracting from it) could yield a new solution to a problem. Redesigning the existing ideas may also yield a new alternative.

6. Use brainstorming to stimulate ideas. Many companies, large and small, use this tactic to increase creativity. In this situation, you and your associates and/ or advisors sit around and record ideas as they pop into your minds. Now, there are no controls here. No matter how silly an idea may sound, it should be given consideration. Some of the greatest inventions were first viewed as useless and wastes of time. The main objective here is to generate as many ideas as possible, without initially considering merit.

> ### Assignment
>
> Always carry a notepad or small tape-recorder to record new ideas that pop into you head. Thinking while driving in your car or jogging, can foster creative thoughts, for example, and you need to record that output the moment it happens.

7. Put yourself in the shoes of the other person (competitor, customer, employee, supplier, and so on) and see if your existing ideas change or new ones emerge. Experts today are telling entrepreneurs to empathize with customers and competitors in order to get a better understanding of the marketplace.

8. Take advantage of unusual circumstances. Unexpected events can provide unexpected opportunities. However, you must be flexible and willing to move quickly.

Epilogue
Keep up to date on the news within your industry and be prepared to strike at opportunities.

143

No Profits Without Risk

If you are looking for total security in an environment without risk, don't expect any dividends in the form of entrepreneurial returns. You must take a risk in order to generate revenues. The more you are willing to risk, the greater the possibility of profits. If you want all of your money protected by the FDIC, or if you are losing sleep over a $500 investment in the stock market, forget about entrepreneurship as a viable employment alternative. You may gripe and complain about your boss and the lousy pay, but you will be happier employed by somebody else as opposed to working for yourself. In other words, you do not have the proper "risk mentality" that it takes to be an entrepreneur. Sorry.

Assignment

If you need that secure paycheck at the end of every week, forget about taking the plunge. Your insecurities will consume you and take away your spirit.

Epilogue

Being an entrepreneur almost always starts out with a period of little or no security. If you can't handle that, bail out now.

144

Protecting Your Flanks

Many entrepreneurs have found success in the marketplace because of their ability to find and exploit niches in particular markets.

Of course, market niches are segmented portions of larger markets that traditionally go unexploited by larger firms for numerous reasons. Sometimes they are never noticed. More likely, those smaller segments are viewed as too costly to pursue and, therefore, will not meet profit expectations.

This is not so anymore, according to the *Wall Street Journal.* Faced with declining domestic and international markets, larger firms are desperately pursuing any profit opportunities that can be found or developed. Many market niches once reserved for small business activity are falling prey to profit-hungry, large corporations. American Express is now providing investment-planning services to individuals and families. Historically, this market has been served by CPAs, self-employed financial planners, and trust departments of local banks.

> ### *Assignment*
>
> Watch out for the big guys in your primary markets. Observe their every move and be prepared to respond to an attack by them on your customer base. Their biggest weakness is customer service, and that is the key to your survival.

You can expect that larger companies will continue to penetrate markets that were once havens for small-business activity.

If they are not involved in start-up operations to exploit market niches, many will purchase existing small firms operating within niches in order to gain a foothold. Also, larger companies are acquiring existing and prospective suppliers (vendors) in an effort to achieve partial or full vertical integration (control of the entire business process from start to finish).

Epilogue

Some entrepreneurs fall victim to the ability of their larger customers to control their destiny. Diversify your customer base as much as possible.

145

Setting up the Innovative and Creative Environment

Many people do not distinguish between creativity and innovation, but there is a difference. Creativity is the process of creating something new or looking at things in a non-traditional way. Innovation deals with applying what has been created or identified in this process. For example, you can invent a new process to reduce manufacturing costs in

Assignment

Nowadays you must provide for an innovative and creative environment if you want to survive. Allow your employees to think "freely and loudly." Experiment with their ideas and apply the ones that work in your business.

your plant. This is a creative endeavor. However, innovation is not advanced unless you apply the new process to your operations. This is a fundamental problem in this country. America is viewed throughout the world as the most creative and inventive nation on the planet. On the other hand, we do not apply all of our creative output to innovative processes.

Epilogue

Other countries procure our creative discoveries and use them in their industrial and business applications more effectively than we do. Countries such as China, India, and Japan are relieved of the R&D cost burdens, yet they can claim to be more innovative.

146

The Secrets

It would seem that successful entrepreneurship hinges on three things. First, you must have a genuine dislike for the boss and\or your job. Second, you need to "stay the course." In other words, persistence pays dividends. Many average people have become successful

Assignment

If you lack any of these traits and cannot compensate for them, don't take the plunge. Save your time and money.

entrepreneurs because of their willingness to persevere. Finally, you must have customer empathy, which is the ability to get close to your market.

Epilogue

If you can't honestly visualize yourself owning a small business, you can't visualize yourself succeeding as an entrepreneur.

147

Ushering in the New Era

More people are pursuing self-employment than at any time in our nation's history. Surprisingly, the largest group starting new businesses are Baby Boomers. As of 2007, 17 percent of Baby Boomers are becoming entrepreneurs. Words such as "serial entrepreneur" are cropping up.

Self-expression, desire for independence, limited job opportunities, and career displacement seem to be the main reasons for the intense interest in entrepreneurship.

The figures seem impressive, but the underlying realities paint a different story. The SBA reports that for every three businesses formed, two will cease to exist. Most simply go out of business for voluntary reasons. Some owners may want to retire or enter a more profitable field while others cannot hack it and move back onto the corporate career track. Ten percent cease operations for involuntary reasons and file for bankruptcy or incur large debts relative to assets and are forced to shut down.

After weighing the statistics, it would seem that about 1/3 of all new businesses eventually fail. Experts contend that failure is not

> ## Assignment
>
> The economy is changing very rapidly and increasing in diversity. Although this produces many entrepreneurial opportunities, it also spawns intense competition and the need to be flexible. You must have the ability, not only to embrace change quickly, but to apply that change to your small business.

bad because it is part of a purification process by which the economic system filters out inefficiencies. This does leave behind debris that has a profound economic and societal impact. Jobs and tax revenues are lost, while some debts are never collected. In addition, those individuals suffering the trauma of defeat can inherit psychological and financial scars that may never disappear, thus inhibiting them from testing the entrepreneurial waters again.

Small-business demise can be attributed to several key factors. Dun & Bradstreet reports that 92 percent of the failures are caused by lack of business acumen. Of course, this directly relates to inadequate business experience and education as well as inappropriate personality traits.

As Baby Boomers, women, minorities, disenfranchised corporate executives, and large companies pursue entrepreneurial industry in an environment of moderate economic growth; competition will increase to new heights. In addition, advances in technology and innovation will shorten the life cycle of many products and services, thus changing consumer demand more frequently. This increases the risk of doing business in the marketplace. Also, as the economy becomes less predictable and more volatile (which it has during the last 10 years), business planning becomes more precarious and less reliable.

> **Epilogue**
>
> *The name of the game is to be prepared for the fight of your life. Planning, flexibility, and your willingness to change will be major factors in driving entrepreneurial success.*

148

War on Markets

I hope that you are now convinced that enhanced entrepreneurial competition will, in fact, cause a war on all marketing fronts. So, what can you do to ensure some degree of entrepreneurial success? Well, the answer is not clear-cut, but one thing is certain: Most individuals who opt for entrepre-

> **Assignment**
>
> Stay alert and flexible. Force yourself to become nimble and quick in response to the big boys trying to steal your markets.

neurship are ill-prepared for the plunge. Of course, this accounts for the large number of small business failures, even in this very robust economy. Adequate investigation, coupled with appropriate education and experience, is your best bet for beating the hell out of your competition.

In reference to competing with large companies, just keep in mind that technological advances and changes in lifestyles will demand more services and also encourage efficiency and creativity in the delivery of these many services. Entrepreneurs are better positioned to meet these specialized demands because they are more flexible than larger firms in mobilizing resources. This ease of movement will enable new and existing entrepreneurial firms to exploit rapid change in service distribution through the application of innovations and new technology.

Epilogue

The Internet is a prime example of this war on markets unfolding in favor of the entrepreneur.

149

U.S. Small Business Administration (SBA)

Assignment

The SBA is the mother load of information and assistance to both prospective entrepreneurs and those already in business. They have an office in most state capitols and larger cities. In larger states there may be several more offices broken into regions of the state. Give them a call.

One of the primary objectives of the U.S. Small Business Administration is to promote the economic well-being of small firms and entrepreneurs. This is partly accomplished by providing an array of business—and managerial—assistance programs that are available upon request. But also keep in mind that the SBA offers valuable financial assistance programs as well, both in terms of direct and guaranteed loans programs.

The best way to assess the capability of the SBA is to access its primary Website at *www.sba.gov* and go from there. You can also call the SBA in Washington, but the best approach is to call the SBA office closest to you. The SBA maintains an office in every state capital.

Epilogue

Free advice is like free food. It tastes better.

150

University Business Development Centers

These organizations are established in tandem with the U.S. Small Business Administration to provide additional counseling services to the small business community. University Business Development Centers (UBDCs) are simply college- or university-based counseling centers utilizing institutional resources, including faculty and students. In addition, these centers muster community involvement and volunteers to accomplish their task of providing help to small firms and

Assignment

UBDCs are great resources. The federal and state governments have been directing lots of money into these centers to coordinate and direct assistance to the entrepreneurial sector. Most major universities have one and many are also located in local community colleges and are easily accessible.

people wanting to start businesses. This is the strongest assistance program provided by the SBA. A UBDC close to you can be found on the SBA Website.

Epilogue

Again: A freebie is worth its weight in gold.

151

SCORE and ACE

Assignment

Although not as potent to the entrepreneurial sector as they once were, these volunteers will fill a gap and you can gain valuable insight from a retired entrepreneur or business executive.

The Service Corps of Retired Executives (SCORE) and the Active Corps of Executives (ACE), both arms of the United States Small Business Administration, provide one-on-one counseling to business operators. SCORE is a group of retired business people who volunteer their services to small businesses through the SBA. ACE is a group of active managers who counsel small-business owners on a voluntary basis. ACE volunteers come from major corporations, trade associations, educational institutions, and professions. The SCORE Website, *www.score.org* will help you identify local chapters and counselors simply by entering your zip code or by the type of expertise.

Epilogue

Nowadays, most SCORE and ACE chapters work directly with the UBDCs to provide a coordinated approach the delivery of assistance services.

Index

A

accounting and financial expertise, hiring someone with, 80

accounts receivable, 133

ACE, 177-178

action, convert ideas into, 92-93

Active Corps of Executives, *see* ACE

"advisory board," form a, 157, 158

articles, writing, 156

B

Baby Boomers, 11

as entrepreneurs, 172

borrowing money, 49-50

from friends and relatives, 51-52

boss, being someone's, 26-27

business insurance, 38

business interruption insurance, 40-41

business plan, 125-126

tweaking your, 152

updating your, 152-153

C

capital, 95

cash and credit, managing, 133-134

cash flow, importance of tracking, 80-81

cash register, computerized,
    31-32
Census Bureau, The, 66
climatic conditions, effect of,
    97-98
Cline, Patsy, 137
communication voids, 20
competition, impact of, 99
competitive consideration, 60-61
computer setup, 33
consumer beliefs, find out, 58-59
consumers, quality-conscious, 129
creative thinking techniques,
    160-161
credit application form, 134
credit as a managing tool,
    trade, 119-120
credit policies, 100
credit, using, 135
creditors, maintaining good
    relationship with, 135
customer
    as king, 71-72
    contact, 156-157
    referrals, 155
    relations policy, 70-71
    sensitivity, 71
customer needs, keeping up
    with, 63
customer, positive referral from
    a, 158

D

data file management, 86
data, organize your, 33-34
debt financing, 54
    sources for, 53-54
decision-maker, are you a
    good, 126-127
decision-making mistakes,
    common, 128-129
decision-making technique, trial
    and error as, 72-73
decision-making, 10 steps to
    wise, 144-145
decisions, two kinds of, 126
deduction, home-office, 17-18
deductions, tax, 16-17
delivery, product, 100-101
distribution, channels of, 95-97

E

economic climate, 101-102
economic times, trying, 162
electrical outlets in home
    office, 13-14
e-mail marketing, 30-31
employee, description of a, 21
employees as assets, 21-22
employees, lying to your, 27-28
employment taxes, 77

Entrepreneurial Life: How to Go for It and Get It, The, 90

entrepreneurial
    motivation, 93-94
    surge, 11

entrepreneurship,
    failed at, 165
    traits of successful, 171-172

equipment use, prioritize, 15

equity financing, 50-51, 54

estimated tax, 76

Ethernet cable, 29

evaluation, periodic, 37

excellence, 129-130

excise tax, 78

extension cords and home office, 14

federal unemployment tax, 77

feedback procedures, 145-146

files, tracking, 16

financial complexities, understand the, 24-25

financial control, maintaining, 103

financial statements, 25

financing, equity, 50-51

financing, two types of, 54

French language, 131

furniture in home office, 14-15

future, planning for the, 67

G

Gardner, John W., 130

get-rich-quick schemes, 141

global warming, beware of, 97-98

goals, set your, 140-141

government regulation, cost of, 103-104

H

Hemphill, Barbara, 81-82

home office
    layout, 14
    space, 13

home office,
    electrical outlets in, 13-14
    furniture in, 14-15

home-based business insurance, 45

home-office deduction, 17-18

human relations, improving, 18-19

I

idea generator, become a, 159

ideas as money in the bank, new, 163-164

ideas, developing, 166-167

important versus urgent tasks, 83

impulsive aspirations, 141-142

impulsive, entrepreneurs as, 79

incentives,
> employee, 22-23
> tax, 22

income tax, 75

industry trends, 104-105

inflation risks, 105-106

innovative and creative environment, creating an, 170-171

insurance for funding, using, 48-49

insurance program, 39-40

insurance rates, 123

insurance,
> business, 38
>> interruption, 40-41
> criminal, 42
> four basics of, 42-43
> home-based business, 45
> Internet business, 45-46
> key person, 41
> malpractice, 46-47

international events, affect of, 106-107

International Trade Administration (ITA), 132

Internet business insurance, 45-46

interruptions and productivity, 84

inventory management, 34-35

inventory, control your, 23-24

investors, 50-51

invoices, 133

IRS agent and your records, 33

IRS Form 1099, 26-27

K

key person insurance, 41

L

labor, expense of, 108

language, global diplomatic, 131

liability,
> general, 43-44
> product/service, 44

licensing, necessity of, 109

listen, learn to, 20

loan package, 49

M

MacKenzie, R. Alee, 88

malpractice insurance, 46-47

managers, successful, 74

managing growth, 136-137

manufacturers, location of, 114

market
> consideration, 59-60
> promotion and strategy, 73-74
> research, 110

segmentation, 60
testing, 63-64
marketing, 55-56
data, 65-66
research, 67-69
marketing fronts, war on, 174-175
marketing program, key
components of, 61-62
markets,
expand upon your, 56-57
judging the, 57-58
materials, raw, 114-115
Medicare tax, 76, 77
metric system, the, 131-132
Microsoft Excel, 34
money, borrowing, 49-50
monitor your business, ways to,
35-36
motivation, entrepreneurial, 93-94

N

nepotism, 25-26
network of colleagues and
associates, form a, 157-158
niches in particular markets,
169-170

O

operations policy, 111
opportunities, new products or
services as, 66-67

opportunity, jump on an, 94
organize yourself, 139
overpayment, 29-30
overseas competition, 107

P

Paar, Jack, 92
PalmPilot, 86
Patton, George, 131
payment terms, 52
persistence and
entrepreneurship, 142-144
presentations, free, 156
pricing products and services, 112
product/service liability, 44
professional associations, 154
profit margins, war on, 122-123

Q

QuickBooks, 30
Quicken, 29

R

R&D, *see* research and
development
recession's warning signals, 102
referral from a customer,

positive, 158

register, computerized, 32

research and development, 115-116

results versus tasks, 85

results, compare actual versus expected, 151

results, hierarchy of, 82-83

retail business owner, 31

risk factor, calculating the, 161-162

risk,

no profits without, 168

understanding, 37

S

SCORE, 177-178

self-employment (SE) tax, 76

Service Corps of Retired Executives, *see* SCORE

Silver, A. David, 90

Small Business Administration (SBA), 51, 57

small-business demise, 173

Social Security tax, 76, 77

software, prepackaged, 34

spam, 31

Spanish language, 131

standard operating procedure (SOP), 111, 127

Stanley, Thomas J., 91

Star Trek, 137

Statistical Abstract of the United States, 65

storage, importance of, 117-118

suppliers as lenders, 52-53

supporters, build a team of, 153-154

survey campaign, 60

sweat equity, 142

T

Taming the Paper Tiger, 81-82

tasks,

important versus urgent, 83

results versus, 85

tax,

estimated, 76

excise, 78

income, 75

tax deductions, 16-17

taxes, employment, 77

technological capital, 148-149

technology,

advances in, 32-33

state of, 116-117

technology assessment planning, 147-148

1099, *see* IRS Form 1099

thank yous, 155

time management, 87

time, prioritizing, 89-90

time-wasters,
> dealing with, 88-89
> putting your finger on, 87

topography, limitations of, 118-119

trial and error as decision-
> making technique, 72-73

U

*U.S. Industry and Trade
> Outlook*, 65

U.S. Small Business Administration
> (SBA), 175-176

U.S. Small Business
> Administration's
> > Office of
> > International
> > Trade, 132

United States Department of
> Labor, 11

University Business Development
> Centers (UBDCs),
> 176-177

V

vendors, 120-121
> information from, 121-122

W

"wage-slave" jobs, 11

warranties as real promises,
> 124-125

Web address, 150

Web-hosting service, 150

Websites, 150-151

wholesalers, 120

Wi-Fi printer, 29

win, desire to, 90-91

window in home office, 13

wireless gateway, 28, 29

wireless, going, 28-29

workers' compensation, 47-48

About the Author

James L. Silvester is president of Dominion Business Resources, a management and financial consulting firm. Previously, Mr. Silvester was president of Business Advisory Systems, Inc., a consulting firm specializing in the development of managerial software systems and consulting services directed to entrepreneurial markets. He also served as vice president of two mortgage companies. Mr. Silvester held a full-time position on the faculty of the Harry F. Byrd School of Business located on the campus of Shenandoah University where he instructed courses in entrepreneurship and was also active as an independent management consultant to small- and medium-sized firms. He holds three earned university degrees from accredited institutions and maintains a membership in the National Honor Society in Business Administration (Delta Mu Delta) and the National Education Society (Phi Delta Kappa). Mr. Silvester has written two best-selling books, *How to Start, Finance, and Operate Your Own Business* and *Secrets of Success in Your Own Business*, with forewords contributed by United States Senator Paul S. Treble. The books, published by Carol Communications of New York City, have been critically acclaimed by the *Ladies Home Journal*, *Entrepreneurial Magazine*, *Boston Herald*, and the *Richmond Times Dispatch*. The works have also been mentioned in *Forbes Magazine* and *Venture Magazine* as well as other media throughout the western hemisphere. More than 400,000 books have sold. His third book, entitled *401 Questions Every Entrepreneur Should Ask*, published by Career Press (Franklin Lakes, New Jersey), arrived on bookshelves in late 2006 and has a foreword contributed by Virginia Governor Tim Kaine.

Mr. Silvester is also a popular seminar speaker. The Senate of the State of Maryland passed a resolution honoring his economic development contribution to Western Maryland. Mr. Silvester resides in Stephens City, Virginia, with his wife, Debbie.